Modern Critical Interpretations

Tennessee Williams's
The Glass Menagerie

Bloom's Modern Critical Interpretations

Adventures of
  Huckleberry Finn
All Quiet on the
  Western Front
Animal Farm
Beloved
Beowulf
Billy Budd, Benito
  Cereno, Bartleby
  the Scrivener, and
  Other Tales
The Bluest Eye
Brave New World
Cat on a Hot Tin Roof
The Catcher in the Rye
Catch-22
Cat's Cradle
The Color Purple
Crime and Punishment
The Crucible
Daisy Miller, The
  Turn of the Screw,
  and Other Tales
David Copperfield
Death of a Salesman
The Divine Comedy
Don Quixote
Dracula
Dubliners
Emma
Fahrenheit 451
A Farewell to Arms
Frankenstein
The General Prologue
  to the Canterbury
  Tales
The Glass Menagerie
The Grapes of Wrath
Great Expectations
The Great Gatsby
Gulliver's Travels

Hamlet
The Handmaid's Tale
Heart of Darkness
I Know Why the
  Caged Bird Sings
The Iliad
The Interpretation of
  Dreams
Invisible Man
Jane Eyre
The Joy Luck Club
Julius Caesar
The Jungle
King Lear
Long Day's Journey
  Into Night
Lord of the Flies
The Lord of the Rings
Macbeth
The Merchant of Venice
The Metamorphosis
A Midsummer Night's
  Dream
Moby-Dick
My Ántonia
Native Son
Night
1984
The Odyssey
Oedipus Rex
The Old Man and
  the Sea
One Flew Over the
  Cuckoo's Nest
One Hundred Years
  of Solitude
Othello
Paradise Lost
The Pardoner's Tale
A Portrait of the Artist
  as a Young Man

Pride and Prejudice
Ragtime
The Red Badge
  of Courage
The Rime of the
  Ancient Mariner
Romeo & Juliet
The Scarlet Letter
A Scholarly Look at
  The Diary of
  Anne Frank
A Separate Peace
Silas Marner
Slaughterhouse-Five
Song of Myself
Song of Solomon
The Sonnets of
  William Shakespeare
Sophie's Choice
The Sound and
  the Fury
The Stranger
A Streetcar Named
  Desire
Sula
The Sun Also Rises
A Tale of Two Cities
The Tales of Poe
The Tempest
Tess of the
  D'Urbervilles
Their Eyes Were
  Watching God
Things Fall Apart
To Kill a Mockingbird
Waiting for Godot
Walden
The Waste Land
White Noise
Wuthering Heights

Tennessee Williams's
The Glass Menagerie

Edited and with an introduction by
Harold Bloom
Sterling Professor of the Humanities
Yale University

Chelsea House Publishers
PHILADELPHIA

© 1988 by Chelsea House Publishers, a subsidiary of
Haights Cross Communications.

Introduction © 1987 by Harold Bloom

Printed and bound in the United States of America

10   9

∞ The paper used in this publication meets the minimum
requirements of the American National Standard for Permanence
of Paper for Printed Library Materials, Z39.48–1984

Library of Congress Cataloging-in-Publication Data
Tennessee Williams's The glass menagerie / edited and with an
    introduction by Harold Bloom.
      p.   cm.—(Modern critical interpretations)
   Bibliography: p.
   Includes index.
   Contents: The glass menagerie revisited / Roger B. Stein—The
glass menagerie, from story to play / Lester A. Beaurline—The
glass menagerie, the revelation of quiet truth / Nancy M. Tischler—
The function of gentleman callers / Elmo Howell—Tennessee
Williams's unicorn broken again / Gilbert Debusscher—Tennessee
Williams, theatre poet in prose / Frank Durham—The revision of
The glass menagerie / Charles S. Watson—The southern gentlewoman /
Signi Lenea Falk—Celebration of a certain courage / C.W.E.
Bigsby—The two Glass menageries, reading edition and acting
edition / Geoffrey Borny—The circle closed / R.B. Parker.
   ISBN 1-55546-052-6
   1. Williams, Tennessee, 1911– Glass menagerie. [1. Williams,
Tennessee, 1911– Glass menagerie. 2. American literature—History
and criticism.] I. Bloom, Harold. II. Series.
PS3545.I5365G537   1988
812'.54—dc19   87-27460
                                                                     CIP
                                                                     AC

Contents

Editor's Note

This book brings together a representative selection of the best critical interpretations of Tennessee Williams's drama *The Glass Menagerie*. The critical essays are reprinted here in the chronological order of their original publication. I am grateful to Daniel Duffy and Carol Clay for their aid to my editing of this volume.

My introduction begins with a consideration of Williams as a dramatic lyrist in the mode of Hart Crane, rather than as a lyrical dramatist in the mode of Chekhov. Roger B. Stein begins the chronological sequence of criticism with an exegesis of the catastrophic bleakness of *The Glass Menagerie*, while Lester A. Beaurline traces its evolution from short story to play.

In her study of *Menagerie*, Nancy M. Tischler sees the drama as Williams's most effective work of theater poetry, after which Elmo Howell contributes a note on the play's Southern background. Gilbert Debusscher analyzes the dramatic function of the image of the unicorn in *Menagerie*, while Frank Durham investigates the play as a poetic drama that chooses prose as its medium.

The differences between *Menagerie*'s two published texts are described by Charles S. Watson, after which Signi Falk explains the play as a study of "the Southern gentlewoman."

C. W. E. Bigsby salutes *Menagerie* as celebrating a gentle courage and compassion, while Geoffrey Borny returns us to the contrasts between the play's reading and acting editions. In this volume's final essay, R. B. Parker reads *Menagerie* as a drama of ambivalence, in which Williams both denies his own earlier life and desires to live it again.

Introduction

I

It is a sad and inexplicable truth that the United States, a dramatic nation, continues to have so limited a literary achievement in the drama. American literature, from Emerson to the present moment, is a distinguished tradition. The poetry of Whitman, Dickinson, Frost, Stevens, Eliot, W. C. Williams, Hart Crane, R. P. Warren, Elizabeth Bishop, down through the generation of my own contemporaries—John Ashbery, James Merrill, A. R. Ammons, and others—has an unquestionable eminence, and takes a vital place in Western literature. Prose fiction, from Hawthorne and Melville on through Mark Twain and Henry James to Cather and Dreiser, Faulkner, Hemingway, Fitzgerald, Nathanael West, and Pynchon, has almost a parallel importance. The line of essayists and critics from Emerson and Thoreau to Kenneth Burke and beyond constitutes another crucial strand of our national letters. But where is the American drama in comparison to all this and in relation to the long cavalcade of Western drama from Aeschylus to Beckett?

The American theater, by the common estimate of its most eminent critics, touches an initial strength with Eugene O'Neill, and then proceeds to the more varied excellences of Thornton Wilder, Tennessee Williams, Arthur Miller, Edward Albee, and Sam Shepard. That sequence is clearly problematical and becomes even more worrisome when we move from playwrights to plays. Which are our dramatic works that matter most? *Long Day's Journey into Night*, certainly; perhaps *The Iceman Cometh;* evidently *A Streetcar Named Desire* and *Death of a Salesman;* perhaps again *The Skin of Our Teeth* and *The Zoo Story*—it is not God's plenty. And I will venture the speculation that our drama palpably is not yet literary enough.

By this I do not just mean that O'Neill writes very badly, or Miller very baldly; they do, but so did Dreiser, and *Sister Carrie* and *An American Tragedy* prevail nevertheless. Nor do I wish to be an American Matthew Arnold (whom I loathe above all other critics) and proclaim that our dramatists simply have not known enough. They know more than enough, and that is part of the trouble.

Literary tradition, as I have come to understand it, masks the agon between past and present as a benign relationship, whether personal or societal. The actual transferences between the force of the literary past and the potential of writing in the present tend to be darker, even if they do not always or altogether follow the defensive patterns of what Sigmund Freud called "family romances." Whether or not an ambivalence, however repressed, towards the past's force is felt by the new writer and is manifested in his work seems to depend entirely upon the ambition and power of the oncoming artist. If he aspires after strength, and can attain it, then he must struggle with both a positive and a negative transference, false connections because necessarily *imagined* ones, between a composite precursor and himself. His principal resource in that agon will be his own native gift for interpretation, or as I am inclined to call it, strong misreading. Revising his precursor, he will create himself, make himself into a kind of changeling, and so he will become, in an illusory but highly pragmatic way, his own father.

The most literary of our major dramatists, and clearly I mean "literary" in a precisely descriptive sense, neither pejorative nor eulogistic, was Tennessee Williams. Wilder, with his intimate connections to *Finnegans Wake* and Gertrude Stein, might seem to dispute this placement, and Wilder was certainly more literate than Williams. But Wilder had a benign relation to his crucial precursor, Joyce, and did not aspire after a destructive strength. Williams did, and suffered the fate he prophesied and desired; the strength destroyed his later work, and his later life, and thus joined itself to the American tradition of self-destructive genius. Williams truly had one precursor only: Hart Crane, the greatest of our lyrical poets, after Whitman and Dickinson, and the most self-destructive figure in our national literature, surpassing all others in this, as in so many regards.

Williams asserted he had other precursors also: D. H. Lawrence and Chekhov. These were outward influences, and benefited Williams well enough, but they were essentially formal, and so not the personal and societal family romance of authentic poetic influence. Hart Crane made Williams into more of a dramatic lyrist, though writing in prose, than the lyrical dramatist that Williams is supposed to have been. Though this influence—perhaps more nearly an identification—helped form *The Glass Menagerie* and (less overtly) *A Streetcar Named Desire,* and in a lesser mode *Summer and Smoke* and *Suddenly Last Summer,* it also led to such disasters of misplaced lyricism as the dreadful *Camino Real* and the dreary *The Night of the Iguana.* (*Cat on a Hot Tin Roof,* one of Williams's best plays, does not seem to me to show any influence of Crane.) Williams's long aesthetic decline covered thirty years, from 1953 to 1983, and reflected the sorrows of a seer who, by his early forties, had outlived his own vision. Hart Crane, self-slain at thirty-two, had set for Williams a High Romantic paradigm that helped cause Williams, his heart as dry as summer dust, to burn to the socket.

II

In Hart Crane's last great Pindaric ode, "The Broken Tower," the poet cries aloud, in a lament that is also a high celebration, the destruction of his battered self by his overwhelming creative gift:

> The bells, I say, the bells break down their tower;
> And swing I know not where. Their tongues engrave
> Membrane through marrow, my long-scattered score
> Of broken intervals . . . And I, their sexton slave!

This Shelleyan and Whitmanian catastrophe creation, or death by inspiration, was cited once by Williams as an omen of Crane's self-immolation. "By the bells breaking down their tower," in Williams's interpretation, Crane meant "the romantic and lyric intensity of his vocation." Gilbert Debusscher has traced the intensity of Crane's effect upon Williams's Romantic and lyric vocation, with particular reference to Tom Wingfield's emergent vocation in *The Glass Menagerie.* More than forty years after its first publication, the play provides an absorbing yet partly disappointing experience of rereading.

A professed "memory play," *The Glass Menagerie* seems to derive its continued if wavering force from its partly repressed representation of the quasi-incestuous and doomed love between Tom Wingfield and his crippled, "exquisitely fragile," ultimately schizophrenic sister, Laura. Incest, subtly termed the most poetical of circumstances by Shelley, is the dynamic of the erotic drive throughout Williams's more vital writings. Powerfully displaced, it is the secret dynamic of what is surely Williams's masterwork, *A Streetcar Named Desire*.

The Glass Menagerie scarcely bothers at such a displacement, and the transparency of the incest motif is at once the play's lyrical strength and, alas, its dramatic weakness. Consider the moment when Williams chooses to end the play, which times Tom's closing speech with Laura's gesture of blowing out the candles:

> TOM: I didn't go to the moon, I went much further—for time is the longest distance between two places. Not long after that I was fired for writing a poem on the lid of a shoebox. I left St. Louis. I descended the steps of this fire escape for a last time and followed, from then on, in my father's footsteps, attempting to find in motion what was lost in space. I traveled around a great deal. The cities swept about me like dead leaves, leaves that were brightly colored but torn away from the branches. I would have stopped, but I was pursued by something. It always came upon me unawares, taking me altogether by surprise. Perhaps it was a familiar bit of music. Perhaps it was only a piece of transparent glass. Perhaps I am walking along a street at night, in some strange city, before I have found companions. I pass the lighted window of a shop where perfume is sold. The window is filled with pieces of colored glass, tiny transparent bottles in delicate colors, like bits of a shattered rainbow. Then all at once my sister touches my shoulder. I turn around and look into her eyes. Oh, Laura, Laura, I tried to leave you behind me, but I am more faithful than I intended to be! I reach for a cigarette, I cross the street, I run into the movies or a bar, I buy a drink, I speak to the nearest stranger— anything that can blow your candles out!

> (*Laura bends over the candles.*)

> For nowadays the world is lit by lightning! Blow out your candles, Laura—and so goodbye. . . .

> (*She blows the candles out.*)

The many parallels between the lives and careers of Williams and Crane stand behind this poignant passage, though it is fascinating that the actual allusions and echoes here are to Shelley's poetry, but then Shelley increasingly appears to be Crane's heroic archetype, and one remembers Robert Lowell's poem where Crane speaks and identifies himself as the Shelley of his age. The cities of aesthetic exile sweep about Wingfield/Williams like the dead, brightly colored leaves of the "Ode to the West Wind," dead leaves that are at once the words of the poet and lost human souls, like the beloved sister Laura.

What pursues Tom is what pursues the Shelleyan Poet of *Alastor*, an avenging daimon or shadow of rejected, sisterly eros that manifests itself in a further Shelleyan metaphor, the shattered, colored transparencies of Shelley's dome of many-colored glass in *Adonais*, the sublime, lyrical elegy for Keats. That dome, Shelley says, is a similitude for life, and its many colors stain the white radiance of Eternity until death tramples the dome into fragments. Williams beautifully revises Shelley's magnificent trope. For Williams, life itself, through memory as its agent, shatters itself and scatters the colored transparencies of the rainbow, which ought to be, but is not, a covenant of hope.

As lyrical prose, this closing speech has its glory, but whether the dramatic effect is legitimate seems questionable. The key sentence, dramatically, is "Oh, Laura, Laura, I tried to leave you behind me, but I am more faithful than I intended to be!" In his descriptive list of the characters, Williams says of his surrogate, Wingfield: "His nature is not remorseless, but to escape from a trap he has to act without pity." What would pity have been? And in what sense is Wingfield more faithful, after all, than he attempted to be?

Williams chooses to end the play as though its dramatic center had been Laura, but every reader and every playgoer knows that every dramatic element in the play emanates out from the mother, Amanda. Dream and its repressions, guilt and desire, have remarkably little to do with the representation of Amanda in the play, and everything to do with her children. The split between dramatist and lyrist in Williams is manifested in the play as a generative divide. Williams's true subject, like Crane's, is the absolute identity between his artistic vocation and his homosexuality. What is lacking in *The Glass Menagerie* is that Williams could not have said of Amanda, what, Flaubert-like, he did say of the heroine of *Streetcar*: "I am Blanche DuBois." There, and there only, Williams could fuse Chekhov and Hart Crane into one.

The Glass Menagerie Revisited: Catastrophe without Violence

Roger B. Stein

In an interview with *Newsweek* in the spring of 1960, Tennessee Williams made an announcement which was bound to be of interest to widespread audiences and critics of the drama alike. He declared that he was "through with what have been called my 'black' plays," that from then on his plays would be free from their earlier accent on the bestiality of man. While not denying that bestiality still existed, Williams declared, "I want to pass the rest of my life believing in other things. For years I was too preoccupied with the destructive impulses. From now on I want to be concerned with the kinder aspects of life." The sweeping quality of the remark was almost Tolstoyan in its rejection of Williams's earlier vision. By contrast to the violence and blackness of the earlier plays, the newer vision seemed to be one of sweetness and light. Williams's last phrase alone reverberates with William Dean Howells's injunction seventy years ago that our novelists "concern themselves with the more smiling aspects of life, which are the more American."

The turn in Williams's career should not have come as a complete shock (even putting aside the question of psychoanalysis). In the foreword to *Sweet Bird of Youth* several years ago, Williams marveled at his audiences' capacity to accept the violence which he was dealing out to them, and by this time violence—of rape, castration, and cannibalism—had become the hallmark of the Williams mode,

From *Western Humanities Review* 28, no. 2 (Spring 1964). ©1964 by the University of Utah.

his way of resolving, or avoiding the real resolution of, the conflicts between his lonely, haunted characters. In that same foreword Williams tried to indicate that violence was not his only dramatic weapon. He divided his dramas into two groups: the violent plays, those which emphasize man's bestiality, and the nonviolent plays. Among the latter he included both *The Glass Menagerie* and the then uncompleted *Period of Adjustment*, because neither depends for its moral justification upon the Aristotelian idea that violence is purged by its poetic representation on a stage and neither play offers us violence as the way to "the release from the sense of meaninglessness and death," which Williams understands to be the object of a work of tragic intention.

The grouping is useful in showing Williams's earlier uneasiness with violence as his sole dramatic technique. Reaching back to his earliest successful drama, Williams grasped again at an approach built not upon the reduction of dramatic situation and motivation to a series of overcharged, sexually violent and symbolically loaded confrontations, where "release" comes from explosion, but upon a quieter pattern of lonely human beings who fail in a variety of ways to make contact with one another and with their universe.

Then, to strengthen one's conviction that Williams was searching for a way out of the pattern of violence which had become his trademark, the 1961 Broadway season gave us *The Night of the Iguana*. Despite the hints of violent action offstage and the explosive personality of its central character, the ex-minister Shannon, the new play offers us through its most sympathetic character, Hannah Jelkes, an ideal of endurance, of quiet strength facing the pain and loneliness of human existence. Her plea at the third act curtain is "Oh God! Can't we stop now? Finally? Please let us. It's so quiet here, now."

The attenuated nature of her cry suggests several observations regarding Williams's work. In the first place, the mood of the play is muffled and elegiac, reminding one, as several critics have noted, of *The Glass Menagerie*. Actually the similarity extends beyond mood to Williams's approach to the problem of the loneliness of defeated souls, his particular area of sensitivity and compassion as playwright. Furthermore, it may be noted that Hannah's cry is framed not solely in human terms, but in terms of man's relation to a God-centered universe. The importance of this has been largely overlooked by Williams's critics heretofore and certainly in their examination of *The Glass Menagerie*.

Finally, both Hannah's speech and *The Night of the Iguana* as a whole help to put *Period of Adjustment* into its very special place in the canon of Williams's work as a deviation from the pattern of his development, a deviation comparable in many ways to that nostalgic comedy, *Ah! Wilderness,* in the career of Eugene O'Neill. For though *Period of Adjustment* is, with *The Glass Menagerie* and *The Night of the Iguana,* a nonviolent play, unlike them it is subtitled "A Serious Comedy," and whatever Williams may mean by "serious," it is clearly comic in its underlying belief in the essential health of society once certain adjustments have been made. This is not to say that the break with his earlier work is complete. Certainly *Period of Adjustment* bears the imprint of the earlier Williams: the concern with homosexuality behind Ralph's fear for his son; the heavy-handed and overinsistent symbolism of the Bates's home being built on a "high point over a cavern"; the parody of the American dream through the spoofing about longhorns and the wild West; and perhaps most important, Williams's tendency to see human conflict too exclusively in sexual terms, whether successfully resolved here, as it was in *The Rose Tattoo,* problematic, as in *Cat on a Hot Tin Roof,* or unresolved and leading to catastrophe, as in *Suddenly Last Summer.* Yet these similarities should not blind us to the more basic shift which occurred and which is implied in the very title of the play. What set this play off from his earlier work, both "violent" and "nonviolent," and from *The Night of the Iguana* was Williams's apparent belief that the lives of four individuals, the well-being of middle-class America, and even the happiness of the Christmas season could be preserved if one was only willing to go through a little "period of adjustment."

Williams's vision in *The Glass Menagerie* of 1945, by contrast, was not one of successful adjustment but of failure, the failure of any manipulation to piece together the fragmented lives of human beings. The essentially sanguine view of the "kinder aspects" which he adopted in 1960, that a little tinkering would set all to rights, was a real if perhaps temporary departure not only from the violent plays but from *The Glass Menagerie*'s searching and poetic vision of catastrophe.

II

When *The Glass Menagerie* first appeared, it was hailed as a major dramatic event (Williams himself later spoke of the play's favorable reception as "The Catastrophe of Success"). In 1948 John

Gassner dubbed Williams the "dramatist of frustration" because Williams had captured with such skill the truncated lives of his characters, caught in a world of their own illusions and unable to break out. Gassner was inclined to see the frustration as that of individuals, though he suggested briefly that the sketched background of the play was social. But the power of *The Glass Menagerie* is even greater than earlier critics have suggested. The full measure of its intensity has yet to be taken, and the contrast between the comic premise of *Period of Adjustment* and the note of endurance in *The Night of the Iguana* is one more reason why we should turn back to his early and perhaps his greatest play to examine not just the surface of frustration but the fullness of its catastrophic vision, a vision not only of individuals who fail to communicate with one another, nor of a society temporarily adrift in a depression, but of man abandoned in the universe.

The means which Williams has used to give form to this vision are symbolic rather than literal. His play about the man who came to dinner and failed to satisfy the expectations of two neurotic women depends not so much upon plot or characterization as upon an undercurrent of allusion, the range of secondary associations which, instead of being in the foreground of dramatic action, serve as a background of ironic commentary on the essentially static surface of this "memory play."

Williams has often asserted, sometimes at rather too great length, that he is the poet in the theater. Again and again he has stressed the inadequacy of the literal significance of words to convey meaning. In his early one-act verse drama, *The Purification,* the son says that "truth is sometimes alluded to in music. / But words are too loosely woven to catch it in." In the afterword to *Camino Real* he went so far as to condemn "words on paper, . . . thoughts and ideas of an author, those shabby things snatched off basement counters at Gimbel's," and to insist that it was the natural symbol for which he was really reaching. In *The Glass Menagerie* this problem is expressed in the poignant interview between Tom and his mother, when Amanda says and Tom agrees that "there's so many things in my heart that I cannot describe to you!" Like his dramatic forebear Chekhov, Williams is constantly faced with the yawning gap between his characters' feelings and their ability to verbalize. In Williams's work this gap often threatens to become an abyss into which the play itself collapses. His critics have been quick to point out when the playwright has substituted strident symbolism for effective dramatic situation. The awkwardness of the screen device proposed for *The Glass Menagerie*, Val's snakeskin jacket and Lady's speech about fig trees and Christmas decorations in *Orpheus Descending*, perhaps the iguana itself in the title of his latest play, and the generally cluttered quality of *Camino Real* come immediately to mind as cases where Williams has failed to develop and then rely upon the dramatic situation and leans upon allusion to carry the meaning rather than dramatic conflict.

The particular excellence of *The Glass Menagerie*, by contrast, is that Williams was able at this one point to sustain both a credible dramatic situation of the anticipation and appearance of the gentleman caller at the same time that he developed with extraordinary skill the secondary level of allusion which gives to the drama its full symbolic significance. The pattern of allusion, the tightness of poetic texture, transforms the pathetic story of the Wingfield family into a calamity of immense proportions.

The structure of the play helped Williams to move away from realistic drama and too great a dependence upon only the literal significance of word or action. His development of *The Glass Menagerie* as a "memory play," organized around Tom's remembrances of things past, gave Williams the freedom to develop the "new plastic theatre" of which he spoke in the author's production notes to the published versions of the play. Lighting, music, and the device of the narrator who is both a commentator on and a part of the series of tableaux which he presents in his search for the meaning of the past all contribute to the play's fluidity, a quality and metaphor which one critic sees as central to Williams's art.

If we move from the play's poet, Tom, to the question of the play's poetry, certainly the clearest and most obvious organizing image is the glass menagerie itself, which embodies the fragility of Laura's world, registers so sensitively any changes in lighting, and stands in vivid contrast to the harshness of the outside world, the so-called world of reality which can shatter it so easily. Dramatically the glass menagerie is the focus of much of the action of the play in much the same way that the garret is the focus of Ibsen's *Wild Duck*. Like the wild duck, the menagerie is almost too strident a symbol. Williams is almost too insistent at times on the parallel between Laura and her menagerie, between the glass unicorn's losing its horn and Jim's impotence when he tries to bring Laura into the "real world." But again like Ibsen, Williams does not hang the entire play upon his title symbol; instead he gives to the play as a whole a poetic texture and a wealth of ironic allusion.

This comes out clearly in his handling of Tom, the narrator, struggling poet, and embryonic Tennessee Williams, whose role has a value far exceeding the range of autobiographical reference which was undoubtedly its starting point. The world of literature is developed through more than the convention of the narrator alone. The play's numerous literary allusions serve both to give a sense of specific detail to the evanescent tableaux-scenes and to reinforce central dramatic issues.

Tom, the poet in the warehouse, is "Shakespeare" to Jim, the gentleman caller. Jim realizes dimly that his friend is that strange creature, the artist, set apart from his fellow men. In the Acting Version [hereafter cited as AV], Williams inserted a few lines during which Amanda tries to adjust the lamp for Tom while he is writing. She chides him: "I know that Milton was blind, but that's not what made him a genius." Like the Shakespeare reference, this is Amanda's recognition of Tom's difference from other men and as such establishes one character's attitude toward another. It also underscores our sense of Amanda's well-meaning meddling in Tom's privacy. Furthermore it works ironically, for it should suggest to the audience Milton's sonnet on his blindness and add to our sense of the conflict between Tom's desire to escape from home and the warehouse and Amanda's belief that "they also serve who only stand and wait." And beyond this, there exists the even broader contrast, inherent in the Milton image, of sight and blindness, of light and darkness. This pattern of imagery is as important to *The Glass Menagerie* as it is to Ibsen's *Wild Duck,* where the conflict between illusion and reality is shaped in terms of visual imagery, of motion toward and away from light of various kinds.

Such an expansion of the range of reference of a single image is neither accidental on the author's part nor implanted there by the critic. It is part of the very texture of the play. The conflict between Tom and his mother is developed in a variety of ways and the world of literature is one battleground. Amanda is outraged at Tom's reading of D. H. Lawrence. When he makes a Lawrencian speech about man's being by instinct "a lover, a hunter, a fighter," she retorts that instinct "belongs to animals! Christian adults don't want it!" (though it should be noted that she is not beyond stuffing Laura's bosom with "Gay Deceivers" before the gentleman caller appears). The barrier to literary communication works both ways. Tom sees the heroines of

Amanda's "literary world" of *The Homemaker's Companion* in Lawrencian terms—"bodies as powerful as Etruscan sculpture"—but the
appeal of this magazine to Amanda and those to whom she sells subscriptions is not the passion, but the fantasy world of romance of the
horsy set on Long Island, a northern version of the fantasy South of
her youth. Where Tom opposes the grim actuality of tenement life
here by an appeal to the pagan and the primitive, Amanda sells the
deceptive view of romance of Bessie May Harper, who "never lets
you down" and "always leaves you with such an uplift" (AV). The
heroines of Bessie May Harper are everything that Amanda hoped to
be and that Laura is not, and even the magazine's title is ironic, for
Amanda has failed as a homemaker and Laura will never be one.

In the Library Edition of the play [hereafter cited as LE],
Amanda ranks Bessie May's latest effort with *Gone With the Wind*,
compounding the irony. The universal desirability of the romantic
Scarlett O'Hara makes Laura seem all the more neglected, and the
fantasy of rebuilding Tara ironically underlines Amanda's loss of her
Blue Mountain girlhood. Furthermore, Amanda Wingfield is not
alone in the nostalgic backward glance to a lost Eden, a fantasy South
that existed only in the American imagination. It is not coincidental
that Margaret Mitchell's Southern romance should have been a best
seller during the depression years. While the allusion to *Gone With the
Wind* clearly sets Amanda apart from her son, it also broadens the
context of Amanda's escape from reality. This escape was one which
most Americans seemed to want to share, and thus her delusion takes
on a larger social significance. Finally one may note that the title
image itself of *Gone With the Wind* underlines the evanescent quality
of this dream and all of the Wingfields' illusions. As such, it points
directly to the last line of the play and Tom's injunction to "blow out
your candles, Laura."

On the level of plot, this widening circle of reference enhances
the credibility of the dramatic situation. Given Amanda's sham version of idealized love and a fantasy past, how could the gentleman
caller's visit be other than a failure? Despite Amanda's dress which is
"historical almost," despite the attempt to live in the nineteenth century when the electric power goes off, Jim is not Rhett Butler but an
"emissary from a world of reality," as Tom calls him, an engaged
twentieth-century man on vacation. The flickering candlelight of
Jim's scene with Laura is not enough to sustain the illusion; at the end
of their scene this illusion collapses and we are left in darkness.

Williams weaves numerous patterns of imagery skillfully within the play. Many converge upon this last scene, and with a care he has not matched since, he directs all of the separate objects and fleeting images toward the central concerns of the drama. After Tom has announced the imminent visit of the gentleman caller, he tries to warn Amanda not to expect too much. He urges her to face the fact that Laura is crippled. Amanda refuses, not only explicitly but also implicitly when she turns thereafter and asks Laura to make a wish on the moon, "a little silver slipper of a moon." The image suggests at once romance, reflected soft light, and (ironically) Laura's limp. The slipper itself foreshadows the later dancing scene between Laura and Jim. At this point Jim destroys the illusion by knocking against the glass menagerie. In the Library Edition there is a further verbal irony in this scene, when Jim kisses Laura, retreats, and then brands himself a "stumblejohn." The gesture of love which she needs so desperately does not heal the crippled Laura and release her from her bondage to her illusions. It shatters her. All the kiss seems to have done is to pass on to Jim, momentarily, Laura's crippled condition. As the ironic use of imagery helps to make clear, the failure of vision at the end of the play is everybody's failure. Even Tom, who thought he was being helpful by bringing Jim home, has illusions which blind him and doom the visit of the gentleman caller to failure. Tom can only escape, leaving Laura and Amanda to withdraw even further into their private worlds.

III

But *The Glass Menagerie* is built upon more than the poignant plot of illusion and frustration in the lives of little people. Williams has given the drama further significance by deepening the losses of individuals and pointing to social and even spiritual catastrophe. The time of the play is 1939, as the narrative frame makes explicit both at the beginning and the end. The life of illusion is not confined to the Wingfields alone. As Tom says, "The huge middle class of America was matriculating in a school for the blind." What he calls the "social background" of the play has tremendous importance. The international backdrop is Guernica and the song America sings is "The World is Waiting for the Sunrise," for the sober truth is that America is still in the Depression and on the brink of war. The note of social disaster runs throughout the drama, fixing the lives of individuals against the larger canvas.

Amanda's anxieties are in large part economic and there is money behind many of her illusions: her mythical suitors were all wealthy men; she hopes to make money by selling subscriptions to the fantasy world of *The Homemaker's Companion;* she computes the money Tom would save by giving up smoking. When Tom complains of the grimness of life in the shoe factory, she replies, "Try and you will SUCCEED!" If this is another of Amanda's illusions, it is one shared by her fellow Americans, for "try and you will succeed" is the traditional motto of the American dream of success, the theme of confident self-reliance canonized in the romances of Horatio Alger.

It is not Amanda, however, but Jim, the emissary from reality, who is the chief spokesman for the American dream. To Jim the warehouse is not a prison but a rung on the ladder toward success. He believes in self-improvement through education, and the lecture on self-confidence which he reads to Laura is part of the equipment of the future executive. Jim is a booster in the American tradition. He is awed by the fortune made in chewing gum and rhapsodizes on the theme of the future material progress of America: "All that remains is for the industry to get itself under way! Full steam—*Knowledge*—Zzzzzp! *Money*—Zzzzzp! *Power!* That's the cycle democracy is built on!"

Yet when the strident theme of success is superimposed upon the lives of the characters, the social irony emerges. Father was not the successful businessman, but a telephone man who "fell in love with long distances." Tom, the substitute father, refuses to pay the light bill, plunges his family into darkness, and then runs out, and Amanda sells subscriptions and brassieres only at the loss of her dignity. Jim's own dream of success seems to have reached its peak in high school. (Williams later explored this theme more fully in *Cat on a Hot Tin Roof.*) The trek upward through the Depression years is disappointing, but the indomitable optimist is not discouraged.

The experience of the 1930s did not turn Williams into a proletarian writer or social realist, but it did open up for him a darker vision of American life which he suggests to his audience but which is denied to his characters, still "matriculating in a school for the blind": a belief that the American dream itself is a sham and a failure. In his essay "The Catastrophe of Success," Williams said that "the Cinderella story is our favorite national myth, the cornerstone of the film industry if not of the Democracy itself" (LE). The social catastrophe inherent in *The Glass Menagerie* lies precisely in the fact that

Laura is *not* Cinderella: the silver slipper does not fit finally, and Jim is not Prince Charming but one of the innumerable Americans who would soon be moving overseas in troop ships. As Tom says at the end, "For nowadays the world is lit by lightning! Blow out your candles, Laura—and so goodbye." The world which had been waiting for the sunrise burst with bombardments instead, and the lives of the Wingfields at the end are absorbed in the larger social tragedy.

Williams goes even further than this, however. The end of the play involves more than just the snuffing out of Laura's hope; it is even more than social tragedy. It is a *Götterdämmerung*. For the candles and the lightning which close the play have appeared together before. We are told by Amanda that the candelabrum "used to be on the altar at the church of the Heavenly Rest. It was melted a little out of shape when the church burnt down. Lightning struck it one spring." Amanda's comment opens up another whole dimension of the play, and points to a catastrophe which readers of *The Glass Menagerie* and Williams's dramas in general have hitherto neglected.

IV

Williams said in 1948 that the dominating premise of his work was "the need for understanding and tenderness and fortitude among individuals trapped by circumstance." To read this statement exclusively in naturalistic terms, however, is to miss much of the force of Williams's dramas. Williams is the grandson of an Episcopal rector in whose house he spent his early years. He is also the inheritor of a Southern religious tradition which includes writers like Faulkner and Robert Penn Warren. Again and again in his plays he comes back to the world of Christian symbolism to describe his individuals "trapped by circumstance." What so often makes the trap horrifying is his recognition, explicit or implicit, that there is no release from it in a world to come. Christian imagery becomes a means of denying Christian belief. In its quieter forms the combination produces cosmic irony; in its most violent manifestations, grotesque parody.

One of his best early one-act plays, *Portrait of a Madonna,* is at once a pathetic portrait of a deranged Southern spinster, precursor of Blanche DuBois of *Streetcar,* and a grotesque parody of the immaculate conception. Miss Collins both believes and denies belief. She has been brought up in the shadow of the Episcopal church but feels she has been abandoned by the church. Her walk in the scorching, merciless sunlight is a kind of passion, punctuated with cries to God, Jesus, and a "merciful Christ in Heaven" who show her no mercy. The recluse who believes herself pregnant wants to educate her imagined child privately, "to make sure that it doesn't grow up in the shadow of the cross and then have to walk along blocks that scorch you with terrible sunlight." The collapse of her belief turns her life into nightmare, as Williams makes amply clear through the tightly woven pattern of Christian reference turned into parody and developed through imagery of light and shadow.

In *Summer and Smoke* the rectory is the home of a deranged woman and the angel in the park which dominates the set brings at the end not heavenly mercy or the "Eternity" inscribed at its base but the traveling salesman. The central irony of this struggle of body and soul is that by the time that Dr. John finally recognizes that human beings do have souls, Alma has given up hope and searches for satisfactions of the body alone. God's mercy comes not in the form of spiritual aid but in sleeping pills. As Alma tells the salesman, "Life is full of little mercies like that, not *big* mercies, but comfortable *little* mercies. And so we are able to keep on going."

In *The Rose Tatoo* Serafina can shed her loneliness and prolonged grief and find love again only after she has blown out the candle under the Madonna's image. The priest is ineffectual and cannot solace her. Only in Mangiacavallo does she find renewed life. *The Night of the Iguana* gives us another ineffectual minister, the Reverend T. Lawrence Shannon. Locked out of his church for heresy and fornication, Shannon rages romantically against the traditional image of God as a "senile delinquent" and wants to preach "God as Lightning and Thunder," in oblivious majesty before the terrors of the human condition. His own suffering is described by Hannah as a "voluptuous crucifixion," and her final appeal to God at the end of the play is only the last link in a chain of imagery of crucifixion and unsuccessful resurrection, of Christian belief gone awry.

Often the religious dimension of the drama is suggested by the time of year. Dr. John in *Summer and Smoke* will be married on Palm Sunday. *Orpheus Descending* reaches its wild climax on Easter Sunday and the lynching of Val Xavier becomes as a result a brutal parody of crucifixion without resurrection. Even *Period of Adjustment* takes place on Christmas Eve.

The religious overtones of *The Glass Menagerie* are even more pervasive. Though they never obscure the literal line of the story or seem self-conscious, as they do in some of the later plays, these over-tones add a dimension to the play which reaches beyond individual pathos and social tragedy. Williams's stage directions clearly indicate his intention. As with Hannah in *The Night of the Iguana,* he tells us that the lighting for Laura should resemble that "used in early reli-gious portraits of female saints or madonnas." The scene where Tom tells his mother that a gentleman caller will appear Williams entitles "Annunciation." The dressing of Laura for the caller's appearance should be "devout and ritualistic." During her scene with Jim she is lit "inwardly with altar candles," and when Jim withdraws after kiss-ing her Williams informs us that the "holy candles in the altar of Laura's face have been snuffed out. There is a look of almost infinite desolation."

Those overtones extend beyond Williams's hints to the director and become a crucial part of the fabric of dramatic action. The first scene in both the Acting Version and the Library Edition of the play opens on this note. In the former, Amanda narrates her "funny expe-rience" of being denied a seat in the Episcopal church because she has not rented a pew. The idea of the Wingfields' exclusion from Chris-tian ceremony is established thus at the outset, and it is underlined by the ensuing talk of digesting food, mastication, and salivary glands. In the Wingfield apartment, eating is an animal process only; it lacks ritual significance. The Library Edition opens with Amanda's call to Tom, "We can't say grace until you come to the table," and then moves on to the question of digestion. The lines are different, but their import is the same. When the gentleman caller comes, the scene is repeated, only this time it is Laura whose absence holds up "grace."

Amanda, who condemns instinct and urges Tom to think in terms of the mind and spirit, as "Christian adults" do, is often char-acterized in Christian terms. Her music, in the Library Edition, is "Ave Maria." As a girl she could only cook angel food cake. She urges Laura, "Possess your soul in patience," and then speaks of her dress for the dinner scene as "resurrected" from a trunk. Her con-stant refrain to Tom is "Rise an' Shine," and she sells subscriptions to her friends by waking them early in the morning and then sym-pathizing with them as "Christian martyrs." Laura is afraid to tell her mother she has left the business school because "when you're disappointed, you get that awful suffering look on your face, like the picture of Jesus' mother in the museum!"

The next picture Laura mentions is the one of Jim in the yearbook; though the context seems secular enough at this point—Jim is a high school hero—his religious function emerges later on. In the "Annunciation" scene, when Amanda learns that the gentleman caller's name is O'Connor, she says, "That, of course, means fish—tomorrow is Friday!" The remark functions not only literally, since Jim is Irish Catholic, but also figuratively, for the fish is the traditional symbol of Christ. In a very real sense both Amanda and Laura are searching for a Savior who will come to help them, to save them, to give their drab lives meaning.

Tom is unable to play this role himself. Though he appears as the angel of the Annunciation, he denies the world of belief and in a bitter speech to his mother calls himself "El Diablo." With him Christian terms appear only as imprecations: "what in Christ's name" or "that God damn Rise and Shine." When Tom returns home drunk one night, he tells Laura of a stage show he has seen which is shot through with Christian symbolism, none of which he perceives. Here the magician, Malvolio, whose name suggests bad will, dislike, or even hate, plays the role of the modern Christ. He performs the miracle of turning water into wine and then goes on to blasphemy by turning the wine into beer and then whiskey. He also produces his proper symbol, the fish, but it is goldfish, as if stained by modern materialism. Most important, perhaps, he escapes from a nailed coffin. But Tom reads the symbolism of this trick in personal terms only. When Laura tries to keep him from awakening Amanda, Tom retorts:

> Goody goody! Pay 'er back for all those "Rise an' Shine's." You know it don't take much intelligence to get yourself into a nailed-up coffin, Laura. But who in hell ever got himself out of one without removing one nail?

The illumination of the father's photograph at this point suggests one answer to this question, but the pattern of Christian imagery in the drama, especially when reinforced here by the "Rise an' Shine" refrain, should suggest to us another answer—the resurrection itself—which Tom's rejection of Christian belief prevents him from seeing.

It remains therefore for Jim to come as the Savior to this Friday night supper. The air of expectancy is great, with the ritualistic dressing of Laura, the tension, and the oppressive heat. Jim's arrival is marked by the coming of rain, but the hopes of fertility and renewal which this might suggest are soon dashed. Laura's attempt to come to the dinner table is a failure, signaled by a clap of thunder, and Tom's muttered grace, "For these and all thy mercies, God's Holy Name be praised," is bitterly ironic, mocked by what follows. The only paradise within reach is Paradise Dance Hall, with its "Waste Land" mood of slow and sensuous rhythms and couples kissing behind ashpits and telephone poles, "the compensation for lives that passed . . . without any change or adventure," as Tom remarks. The failure of electric power after dinner—previsioning the blackout of the world—leads to Amanda's joking question, "Where was Moses when the lights went off?" This suggests another savior who would lead his people from the desert into the promised land, but the answer to her question is "In the dark."

Jim's attempt to play the modern savior is an abysmal failure. In the after-dinner scene, he offers Laura the sacrament—wine and "life-savers," in this case—and a Dale Carnegie version of the Sermon on the Mount—self-help rather than divine help—but to no avail. At the end of the play Laura and Amanda are, as the joke bitterly reminds us, "in the dark," and Tom's last lines announce the final failure, the infinite desolation: "For nowadays the world is lit by lightning. Blow out your candles, Laura—and so goodbye."

Here, as elsewhere in his plays, Williams draws upon his frightened characters' preference for soft candlelight to harsh daylight or electric bulbs, not only because it serves him dramaturgically to establish his conception of a new plastic theater where evanescent characters and images flicker across the stage momentarily, but also because his characters so often want to withdraw from the blinding light of reality into the softer world of illusion. At the end of *The Glass Menagerie*, however, the blackout is even more catastrophic, for it not only develops the Laura of Tom's memory and serves as another reminder of the blackout of war which shrouds the world: it is also the denial of any final "Rise an' Shine" for these frail creatures. The church has been struck by lightning, and all hope of resurrection has been lost in this damned universe where belief turns into metaphor, where man seems abandoned by his God, and where the echoes of prayer are heard only in blasphemy or irony. The bleakness of Williams's vision in *The Glass Menagerie* is complete. If Tom is released finally, it is in the words of Job, "And I only am escaped alone to tell thee." It is as the author's surrogate, as writer and chronicler of catastrophe, that he emerges at the end.

The theatre of
Tennessee Williams
Vol. 2

$12.54 W:1

Please

The Glass Menagerie:
From Story to Play

Lester A. Beaurline

"Not even daring to stretch her small hands out!—nobody, not even the rain, has such small hands." Tennessee Williams scrawled these words from e. e. cummings at the top of the last page of *The Glass Menagerie* sometime after finishing the one-act play that was to grow into his first successful work. The quotation suggests the gentle, elegiac tone that he tried to attain, and since the last half of the passage survived as the play's epigraph, it apparently expressed Williams's later feelings too. The fragile pathos of Laura Wingfield's life was Williams's original inspiration in his short story "Portrait of a Girl in Glass," and theater audiences continue to respond to the basic human appeal of the play.

In "Portrait" the narrator feels compassion for Laura, who "made no positive motion toward the world but stood at the edge of the water, so to speak, with feet that anticipated too much cold to move." In this early story we can already recognize Williams's other trademarks: the theme of Tom's flight from "a dead but beautiful past into a live but ugly and meaningless present" (William Sharp), the images of leaves torn from their branches, the hundreds of little transparent pieces of glass, the tired old music of the dead past, and the emotional undercurrent of sexual passion roaring through the entire story. These themes, I suppose, show Williams's kinship with D. H. Lawrence; and Tom, no doubt, suggests the figure of Paul

From *Modern Drama* 8, no. 2 (September 1965). ©1965 by A. C. Edwards.

Morrell or Aaron Sisson. But the later revisions show Williams's real talents as a playwright, none of which he inherits from Lawrence: his breadth of sympathy, his sense of humor, his brilliant dialogue, and his talent for building highly charged dramatic scenes.

Evidence survives for at least four stages in the composition of *The Glass Menagerie:* (1) The sixteen-page story entitled "Portrait of a Girl in Glass" (written before 1943 and published in *One Arm and Other Stories*, 1948), where attention is on Laura, the narrator's sister.

(2) A sixty-page one-act play in five scenes, of which twenty-one pages survive in the C. Waller Barrett Library at the University of Virginia. It is clear from the existing fragments that Williams had the main lines of his play firmly in hand at this stage. Here the clash between Tom and Amanda, the painful relationship between Amanda and Laura, and the contrast between Jim and Tom have become as important as Laura herself. This script was probably written before Williams went to California to work on a movie script in 1943 and before he worked up a synopsis for a film named *The Gentleman Caller* (Nancy M. Tischler, *Tennessee Williams*).

(3) A 105-page play manuscript, now in the C. Waller Barrett Library at the University of Virginia. This complex document contains ten kinds of paper, is written on at least six different typewriters, and has four different kinds of handwritten pencil or ink revisions. It may represent about eight to ten layers of revision, but for the sake of clarity, I will refer to only the final stage of the third version: the manuscript as it stood when Williams sent it off to his agent in the fall of 1943. He called this the Reading Version, and it is very close to the Random House edition, published in 1945 and reprinted by New Directions in 1949. However, this printed edition (which unfortunately has gotten into the college anthologies) contains several errors and a few alterations. The long version of the manuscript is in seven scenes and is a development and expansion of episodes in the one-act version. At this stage the major emphasis in the play is on memory, Tom's memory. It is a play about growing up as Tom must recognize the fatal choice between Laura's glass animals and Jim's gross materialism.

(4) The Acting Version, published by the Dramatists Play Service in 1948 (and revised again sometime in the mid-fifties). This purports to be "a faithful indication of the way the play was produced in New York and on the road" by the original company. Many changes have been made in the stage directions and details of

the dialogue. One new scene was added, and over 1100 verbal changes appear in the dialogue alone. I think that Williams is now finished with the play and that the fourth version represents his final intentions. Therefore a responsible editor of an anthology should *not* reprint the old Reading Version, and a critic ignores the Acting Version at his peril.

Changes in Tom's last speech epitomize all the revision in the play, so it is worth examining a long passage that closes the "Girl in Glass."

> Not very long after that I lost my job at the warehouse. I was fired for writing a poem on the lid of a shoe-box. I left Saint Louis and took to moving around. The cities swept about me like dead leaves, leaves that were brightly colored but torn away from the branches. My nature changed. I grew to be firm and sufficient.
>
> In five years' time I had nearly forgotten home. I had to forget it, I couldn't carry it with me. But once in a while, usually in a strange town before I have found companions, the shell of deliberate hardness is broken through. A door comes softly and irresistibly open. I hear the tired old music my unknown father left in the place he abandoned as faithlessly as I. I see the faint and sorrowful radiance of the glass, hundreds of little transparent pieces of it in very delicate colors. I hold my breath, for if my sister's face appears among them—the night is hers!

In the second draft (the one-act version), Williams heightened Tom's emotional tension between his necessary cruelty and his affection for the ones he is hurting. His cruel side comes out when he says, "Then I escaped. Without a word of goodbye, I descended the steps of the fire-escape for the last time." The incestuous implications of the speech become more explicit: "In five years' time I have nearly forgotten home. But there are nights when memory is stronger. I cannot hold my shoulder to the door, the door comes softly but irresistibly open. . . . I hold my breath. I reach for a cigarette. I buy a drink, I speak to the nearest stranger. For if that vision goes on growing clearer, the mist will divide upon my sister's face, watching gently and daring to ask for nothing. Then it's too much: my manhood is undone and the night is hers."

In the third version, the speech is more integrated with the scene. Amanda had just shouted at him, "Go then! Then go to the moon!—you selfish dreamer." So Tom begins his epilogue with "I didn't go to the moon. I went much further—for time is the longest distance between two places." (We should recall that Amanda had asked Laura to wish on the moon before the gentleman caller came.) Another unifying detail was added at the end. Laura, in pantomime, blows out the candles, which like the moon have come to suggest her hopes, the romantic half-light, similar to the glow that came across the alley from the Paradise Ballroom. She had already blown out her candles in the second version, but in the third, Tom says, "anything that can blow your candles out! (LAURA *bends over the candles.*) Blow out your candles, Laura!—for nowadays the world is lit by lightning! Blow out your candles, Laura,—and so goodbye. . . . (*She blows the candles out. The scene dissolves.*)" So the dialogue and action reinforce each other.

Also in the third version Tom gives a more concrete impression of the memory of his sister. He suggests a little dramatic scene where he is no longer in a bedroom with his shoulder to the door. Perhaps the lines from e. e. cummings stimulated an impression of out-of-doors rather than a bedroom. Toms says,

> Perhaps I am walking along a street at night, in some strange city, before I have found companions. I pass the lighted window of a shop where perfume is sold. The window is filled with pieces of colored glass, tiny transparent bottles in delicate colors, like bits of a shattered rainbow.
>
> Then all at once my sister touches my shoulder. I turn around and look into her eyes. . . .
>
> Oh, Laura, Laura, I tried to leave you behind me, but I am more faithful than I intended to be!

The fourth or Acting Version emphasizes Tom's maturity and cruelty even more; now Tom leaves out all mention of his being fired from his job at the warehouse. The impression is that he voluntarily left home—to join the merchant marine. His costume, on stage, has become a pea jacket and a watch-cap, again combining the dialogue and the spectacle.

Joining the merchant marine represents his escape into freedom, his escape from a box; and the second and third versions for the whole play show the regular growth of this theme. To draw the light away from the relations of Tom and Laura and towards an inevitable clash between Tom and Amanda, Williams wrote a long argument into the early scenes. Amanda accuses Tom of being selfish, not caring for his poor sister, and Tom replies vehemently. The first half of this passage is, as many other speeches in the manuscript, in loose blank verse, which the printed texts obscure.

> Listen! You think I'm *crazy* about the *warehouse*?
> You think I'm in love with the Continental Shoemakers?
> You think I want to spend fifty-five *years* down there in
> that —*celotex interior!* with—*fluorescent*—*tubes?!*
> Look! I'd rather somebody picked up a crow-bar and
> battered out my brains—than go back mornings! I GO!
> Everytime you come in yelling that God damn "*Rise and
> Shine! Rise and Shine!*" I say to myself, "How *lucky dead
> people are!*"

As J. L. Styan (*Elements of Drama*) observed, good dramatic speech has had a "specific pressure put on it"; it is economical because it functions in several ways at the same time. This speech not only furthers the action, but it characterizes Tom, the frustrated poet, who sees his work and his home as a box where he endures a living death, surrounded by phoniness and clichés. But the audience is also aware of Amanda's reaction, because we have just seen how she suffers, in her comitragic telephone conversations, while she tries to sell magazines in order to put her daughter through business college. Meantime Laura spends her days walking in the park or polishing her glass. Neither does Williams let us forget Laura during the big argument. In the third version, a spotlight shines upon her tense body; in the fourth version, she stands in the living room, at the door of the dining room, overhearing the whole exchange. Thus she is between the audience and the action in the dining room.

Then before Tom storms out of the apartment, he flings his coat across the room, *"it strikes against the shelf of Laura's glass collection, there is a tinkle of shattering glass. Laura cries out as if wounded."* This stage business is an obvious parallel with the accident that occurs in the next act at the end of Laura and Jim's dance, when the little glass unicorn is broken, just before Jim reveals that he is engaged to marry. He can never call on Laura again.

Scene 4, the only new scene that was written for the Acting Version (but printed in the Random House edition and absent from the Barrett manuscript) also emphasizes the choice that Tom has between death and escape. Tom has come home from the movies, where he gets his adventure, and he describes the magician in the stage show.

> But the wonderfullest trick of all was the coffin trick. We nailed him into a coffin and he got out of the coffin without removing one nail. There is a trick that would come in handy for me—get out of this 2 by 4 situation. . . . You know it don't take much intelligence to get yourself into a nailed-up coffin, Laura. But who in hell ever got himself out of one without removing one nail? (*As an answer, the father's grinning photograph lights up.*)

There are a hundred ways that the body of the play depicts Tom's awareness of the essential hopelessness of the Wingfield family and the essential deadness of their beautiful memories. I will not explain how each detail came into the script; two more examples will have to suffice. One of the greatest moments in modern theater occurs when Amanda comes on stage to greet Laura's gentleman caller. Nobody says a word for a few seconds; everyone's eyes are fixed on Amanda's dress—the old ball dress that she wore when she led the cotillion years ago. Before age had yellowed this dress she had twice won the cakewalk, and she had worn it to the Governor's ball in Jackson. The dress, at this moment, suggests the utter futility of Amanda's efforts to find a husband for her daughter. She defeats her own purposes; she cannot resist pretending that the gentleman caller has come to call on her, just as seventeen of them came one afternoon on Blue Mountain. Tom is shocked and embarrassed. The grotesque sight leaves Jim speechless, and he is a young man proud of his high-school training in public speaking. Meanwhile Laura lies in her bedroom, sick with fear.

Mr. Williams did not achieve such a theatrical triumph by writing with his guts or by pouring out his uncontrolled libido. In the short story, he tried to make Laura pathetic by dressing her in one of her mother's old gowns, and Tom is momentarily surprised by her appearance when she opens the door. In the one-act version, Amanda's memories of Blue Mountain are written into the script, and Laura is furnished with a new dress, but now she is lame. By the third version (possibly in the second, too, but I cannot be sure because the relevant pages of the second version do not survive), Amanda wears the old dress and becomes a coquette. In the fourth version, Williams softens the effect slightly and adds a little more to the irony by a brief exchange between Tom and his mother. At the peak of Tom's embarrassment, after the pregnant pause, he says:

> Mother, you look so pretty.
> AMANDA: You know, that's the first compliment you ever
> paid me. I wish you'd look pleasant when you're
> about to say something pleasant, so I could expect it.

Then Amanda swings into her girlish chatter. These last additions seem to assure the audience that Tom is genuinely shocked but that he is trying to cover up his feelings. At the same time the audience has to have evidence that Amanda is not completely out of her mind. She can still recognize a hollow compliment, and she can return the jibe.

By typical use of his dramatic talents, Williams makes the audience conscious of several characters' feelings at the same time, like a juggler keeping four balls in the air. Each revision puts another ball in the air or increases the specific pressure. We are never allowed to forget the tension between Tom and his mother, and the scene strongly suggests that Laura's anxiety and withdrawal may have been caused by her aggressive mother. The final image of Amanda in the epilogue is that of a comforter and protector of Laura. She is dignified and tragic. But she is most vividly depicted in the middle of the play as a vigorous, silly, and pathetic old woman. Fearing that her daughter might become an old maid, she arranges the visit of a gentleman caller. Yet, she cannot resist the temptation to smother her daughter and relive her Blue Mountain days; she vicariously seduces the man herself. She has to keep bringing the dead but beautiful past into the present; Tom must go into the ugly but live future. He must break out of the coffin and leave his sister behind in darkness.

The transmutations of Jim O'Connor illustrate Mr. Williams's talent for depicting minor characters. At the start, Jim had a warm masculine nature; he was a potential lover and a Lawrencian hero. "Jim was a big red-haired Irishman who had the scrubbed and polished look of well-kept chinaware. His big square hands seemed to have a direct and very innocent hunger for touching friends. He was always clapping them on your arms or shoulders and they burned through the cloth of your shirt like plates taken out of an oven."

In the one-act version, Jim becomes slightly hollow when he tries to persuade Tom to study public speaking. Then, in the Reading

Version, Jim assimilates some of the play's nostalgic tone when he becomes an ex-high-school hero. The distracting homosexual suggestions disappear, and now Tom was "valuable to him as someone who could remember his former glory, who had seen him win basketball games and the silver cup in debating." On the edge of failure, Jim seems to put on his hearty good nature. He is more often named the "gentleman caller" than Jim O'Connor, a detail that helps to transform him into an idea in the head of Amanda, just as Laura becomes an image of "Blue-roses" in his mind. Also in the Reading Version Jim first talks enthusiastically about the world of the present and future—the world that Amanda and Laura cannot enter. When he should be romancing with Laura, he orates on the Wrigley Building, the Century of Progress, and the future of television. "I wish to be ready to go up right along with it. Therefore I'm planning to get in on the ground floor. In fact I've already made the right connections and all that remains is for the industry itself to get under way! Full steam—(*His eyes are starry.*) *Knowledge*—Zzzzzp! *Money*—Zzzzzp!—*Power*! That's the cycle democracy is built on!" He clumsily breaks Laura's unicorn, and he awkwardly kisses her.

Jim finally impresses us as a dehumanized figure, an unromantic voice of power and cliché; his sex appeal has been carefully removed, and his insensitive words and power of positive thinking take its place. Consequently, with every change he suits Laura less and less, and he embodies Tom's "celotex interior" more and more. In the finished play, Amanda's mental projection of the old-fashioned gentleman caller reveals him to be Tom's brute reality.

Other important changes are found in the stage directions, especially the visual images and printed legends that Williams experimented with and rejected—wisely, I think. One legend, "A Souvenir," survives in the fragments of the one-act play (at the beginning of what was eventually scene 8), and the earliest forms of the Reading Version show an attempted use of a blackboard on which Tom wrote in chalk such things as *"Blue Roses"* (scene 2), *"Campaign"* (scene 3), and *"Où sont les Neiges d'antan"* (scene 1). The completed Reading Version projected these legends by means of the much discussed "screen device," possibly conceived in the film synopsis that preceded the Reading Version. Williams said, "The legend or image upon the screen will strengthen the effect of what is merely allusion [sic] in the writing and allow the primary point to be made more simply and lightly than if the entire responsibility were on the spoken lines." The real weakness of the device lies in the author's anxiousness and small confidence in his audience. "In an episodic play, such as this, the basic structure or narrative line may be observed from the audience; the effect may seem fragmentary rather than architectural. This may not be the fault of the play so much as a lack of attention in the audience." And I suspect that if the screen device has ever been tried, it distracted the audience from the actors, just as the lighting can distract unless it is used sparingly. Father's lighted picture seems to work once or twice, but I doubt if similar mechanical marvels add to the unified effect. At any rate, Williams says he does not regret the omission of the screen device in the first New York production, because he saw that Laurette Taylor's powerful performance "made it suitable to have the utmost simplicity in physical production." Jo Mielziner's two scrims no doubt also helped persuade him. An air of unreality is one thing but pretentious pointing out of meaning is another.

Williams's most successful revisions of stage directions unobtrusively change the story's matter-of-fact tone into memory. The narrator of the story becomes the presenter of the play, and significant stage properties appear in the big scene: the blasted candelabra from the altar of the Church of the Heavenly Rest, the ice cream, fruit punch, and macaroons. In the Reading Version the ice cream was replaced with dandelion wine (for a mock communion?), and Amanda "baptizes" herself with lemonade—all of which contributes to the vague religious impression of the scene. No one explicitly defines the meaning of these symbols, but they quietly suggest that the events represent Laura's pitiful initiation rites; this is as close as she will ever come to the altar of love, because Jim is no Savior. She must blow her candles out. The empty ceremony is over.

The Glass Menagerie: The Revelation of Quiet Truth

Nancy M. Tischler

Never a good critic of his own work, [Tennessee] Williams later looked back at both *Battle of Angels* and *The Glass Menagerie* and said of the first, "That play was, of course, a much better play than this one. The thing is, you can't mix up sex and religion, as I did in *Battle of Angels*, but you can always write safely about mothers." He had worked so hard on the complex plot for his first Broadway play that the simple story of the second made it appear inferior. Authors seldom perceive that difficulty in composition bears little relation to the merit of the finished product. The troublesome play is like a maimed or difficult child that one loves all the more for the trouble he causes. To anyone but the writer himself, the fact that *The Glass Menagerie* was so easy to write suggests something of its truth, its naturalness, and its artistry.

The mother Williams had chosen to write about in *The Glass Menagerie* was, naturally, his own. The story is that of his last years in St. Louis—the Depression, "when the huge middle class of America was matriculating in a school for the blind. Their eyes had failed them, or they had failed their eyes, and so they were having their fingers pressed forcibly down on the fiery Braille alphabet of a dissolving economy." Tom, the hero, is working days at the shoe factory and writing nights in his stuffy room or going to the movies. The father of the play, who deserted the family some years earlier,

From *Tennessee Williams: Rebellious Puritan*. ©1961 by Nancy M. Tischler. The Citadel Press.

having been a telephone man who fell in love with long distances, haunts the scene pleasantly in the form of an ineluctably smiling photograph. The mother, Amanda Wingfield, is trying to hold the family together and to steer her children into more practical paths than those she has followed herself, for she is a disillusioned romantic turned evangelical realist.

She lectures Tom on the merits of tending to business. By soliciting magazine subscriptions over the phone she finances a secretarial course in business school for Laura, her daughter. When Amanda finds that Laura is too nervous to learn to type, she decides that the girl must marry. This requires exposing her to an eligible bachelor, whom, to his consternation, Tom is to provide. Tom finally approaches Jim O'Connor, a fellow employee at the shoe factory, and invites him to dinner. Overdoing it, as usual, Amanda sets about redecorating the house and revising her daughter's dress and personality. Her frenzy makes the trio increasingly tense as they await the approach of Jim, the gentleman caller.

Jim had known Laura in high school and has been her idol for years. His nice manners appeal to Amanda. The dinner, consequently, proceeds beautifully, with only one slight interruption: the lights go off because Tom has spent the electric-bill money. Candlelight, however, suffices.

After dinner, Amanda hauls her son to the kitchen to provide privacy to the young couple whom this obvious maneuver reduces to painful embarrassment. Very shortly, though, Jim's good nature melts Laura's shyness, and she finds herself sitting on the floor with him chatting cozily by candlelight, sipping dandelion wine. They talk of Jim's ambitions in electrodynamics and of his night-school courses. Then they turn to a discussion of Laura's collection of tiny glass animals and of her prize, a little unicorn. When, a few minutes later, they start to dance, Jim stumbles and breaks the horn off the little animal. Laura cradles her pet in her palm, musing that he is better off without his horn, for now he can be normal, like the other animals of the menagerie.

In this glimpse, we realize that sweet, simple Laura believes in these little creatures with the same eagerness that Jim believes in electrodynamics. Finally, in a clumsy effort to apply his half-digested understanding of psychology, Jim decides that Laura has an inferiority complex and that he can cure it with a kiss. Then, horrified at what his action might suggest to this fuzzily romantic girl, he blurts out the secret that he is engaged. Laura, strangely enough, seems to be no more hurt by this clumsiness than by the breaking of the unicorn. Rather, on learning that her gentleman caller is not an eligible bachelor, she smiles stoically and gives him her now-hornless unicorn as a souvenir.

The tender mood is broken by the gay entrance of Amanda, bearing a pitcher of lemonade and singing a cruelly appropriate song about lemonade and old maids. Jim, finally understanding why he was invited, takes this moment to explain to Amanda that he plans to marry soon. Then he beats a hasty retreat. Amanda turns spittingly upon her son, who in turn stalks off to the movies. She screams after him that he can "go to the moon" since he is nothing but a selfish dreamer anyway. The final scene is a *tableau vivant* of Amanda, looking dignified and beautiful, comforting her daughter while Tom explains that he eventually escaped from the women to follow the pattern of his roving father. This simple story, turning on a dinner party given by a Southern family for an outsider whom they hope to match with their unmarried daughter and the character revelations that occur in its course, constitutes Tennessee Williams's most fragile and lovely play.

In some ways, *The Glass Menagerie* is a variation of the battle-of-angels theme. Tom expresses the same need to escape the nailed-up coffin of his restricted existence that Val expresses in the earlier play; but Tom seems to be more conscious of a corresponding loss that such freedom implies. He rejects the possessive love of his family because he can accept it only by shouldering the responsibility and accepting the imprisonment that go with it. The rejection of this relationship gives him pain, however, as his proposed desertion of Myra apparently did not give Val. This is a more realistic evaluation of human needs and yearnings. The characters also are more realistic. Although Tom and the others in *The Glass Menagerie* may represent attitudes toward life, none are personified abstractions. There is no Jabe to represent death. A subtler type of characterization combined with a simpler, less melodramatic story yields a far more artistic product.

One of the chief characters is sketched only by implication. The father of the Wingfield family hovers over the scene, although he never appears on stage at all. An enlarged photograph of him, which the spotlight occasionally illuminates, reminds us of his part in the formation of the dramatic situation. It is the picture of a handsome young man in a doughboy's cap. Though deeply hurt by his desertion, Amanda considers her erstwhile husband the embodiment of romance, associating him with that time in her life when the house in Blue Mountain was filled with gentleman callers and jonquils. (Blue Mountain is Mr. Williams's poetic name for Clarksdale, the standard symbol in his plays for romantic, happy youth.) Not having seen her husband growing old and ugly enables her to preserve her romantic image of him. That the father does not appear directly in the play suggests that Tennessee Williams could not view him with sufficient objectivity to portray him. The photograph apparently represents the standard view the outside world caught of the gay, soldierly C. C. Williams, whom his son hated so much that the sweetness would have gone out of the play if he had been included.

To Tom Wingfield, on the other hand, his father represents escape. He says of him, in the narrator's preface to the story, "He was a telephone man who fell in love with long distances; he gave up his job with the telephone company and skipped the light fantastic out of town." Then follows a hinted admiration of his romantic disappearance: "The last we heard of him was a picture post-card from Mazatlan, on the Pacific coast of Mexico, containing a message of two words—'Hello Good-bye!' and no address." Tom's interest in his father's wanderlust, at the beginning of the play, prepares us for Tom's departure at its end. The picture itself, an enlarged photograph of Tom's own face, further emphasizes the similarities of their natures. Thus, while the father still personifies love to the romantic memory of the middle-aged Amanda, he symbolizes another kind of romance to his son—the romance of escape and adventure.

In discarding the real father's part, Tennessee Williams found it necessary to endow the mother with some masculine practicality, thus giving Amanda Wingfield an exceedingly complex personality. Like Myra of *Battle of Angels*, she has her past to recall and her present to endure. One had Moon Lake and love in the vineyard, the other Blue Mountain and gentleman callers. Amanda is, obviously, far more the lady, the Southern aristocrat, than the more voluptuous Myra. The only way Amanda can live with ugly reality is to retreat into her memories; there is no sexual solution for her. Her clothes, her speech, and her ideals for her children declare her belief in the past and her rejection of the present. As the author says of Amanda, "She is not paranoiac, but her life is paranoia."

The feature of this woman which makes her a more admirable

character than the later Blanche of *Streetcar* is the anomalous element of practicality encased in her romantic girlishness. Although she has approached much of her life unrealistically, her plans for her children and her understanding of their shortcomings are grimly realistic. Even when refusing to admit it, she knows Laura will never marry. She then tries to find Laura a protective corner of the business world. When this fails, she rallies for the valiant but hopeless attempt to marry the girl off. This second failure, we feel, is less tragic for the daughter than for the mother. (My use of the term *tragic* corresponds with Mr. Williams's. I do not see most of his people.as having the stature of the classical or neoclassical tragic heroes, but in their symbolic value they do express heroism. Their status and their values are not so exalted as in the older plays. They are more realistic and pathetic than the traditional hero was allowed to be.)

Here we see the quality that Williams suggests from the beginning as the key to Amanda's character—her heroism. This, rather than her romantic turn, is her attraction. At the end of the play, when Tom has left, Amanda bends over Laura, huddled upon the sofa, to comfort her. By then, the audience realizes that Amanda herself is in greater need of this sympathy than the quietly resigned Laura. "Now that we cannot hear the mother's speech," says Williams, "her silliness is gone and she has dignity and tragic beauty."

We see this heroism in Amanda in her relations with Tom as well as with the more delicate and more romantic Laura. Although Tom understands the personality of his mother better than any other character in the story, he is more visionary and irresponsible than she is. He cannot see or accept the necessities of their life. Because of this and her previous experience with a romantic husband, she discourages Tom's attempts at a poetic or a nautical career. She returns the D. H. Lawrence novel to the library and nags at him whenever he escapes to a movie. She prods him to take an interest in practical things, like Jim's night classes in electrodynamics. Here, as with her daughter, she is doomed to failure. Consequently, her final line is, "Go, then! Then go to the moon—you selfish dreamer!" Amanda is better able to speak these words with understanding because she shares his yearnings. Her dream has been smashed by reality but has not been forgotten.

Tom is a poet who is desperately unhappy in his warehouse job, and, as yet, frustrated in his poetry. Since Tennessee Williams knows something of this not-very-tender trap, he speaks with feeling about the afflictions of the machine age. Believing that many, like himself, are poetic rather than mechanistic, he considers surrender to the machine a perversion of man's nature. His escape, heartless though it may seem, is a "necessary and wholesome measure of self-preservation" (as John Gassner expresses it).

Laura, like Rose, obviously can't escape into movies, alcohol, or literature; she simply isn't that violent or decisive. Her retreat is into a world of glass and music. Her father's old phonograph records provide her with escape that the unfamiliar new tunes can't provide. In the short story out of which the play grew, "Portrait of a Girl in Glass," Tom occasionally brings new records to his sister, but she seldom cares for them because they remind her too much of "the noisy tragedies in Death Valley or the speed-drills at the business college." Her collection of glass absorbs her time. She spends hours polishing the tiny animals that are as delicate and fragile as she.

Unable to adapt to the modern scene of electrodynamics, she lives in a world of candlelight and fantasy. The encounter with the machine age is brief and useless. Laura could no more learn to type than Tom could ever come to like his job. Yet, unlike Tom, Laura seems not to feel the ugliness and entombment of their lives. Incapable of his violence, she never steps into the world for fear it would be impossible to bear. She merely stands at the brink and catches what she can of its beauty without becoming a part of it—a lovely picture of the simple Rose, who all through her brother's life has represented to him everything good and beautiful, soft and gentle.

Laura's early surrender is explained at the opening of the play by an allusion to an illness in childhood which left her crippled, one leg slightly shorter than the other and held in a brace (a physical parallel to Rose's mental affliction). The author explains, "Stemming from this, Laura's separation increases till she is like a piece of her own glass collection, too exquisitely fragile to move from the shelf."

Her mother is both Laura's disease and her brace. It is Amanda's forcefulness that allows Laura to walk at all, but it is also Amanda's example that discourages Laura from walking naturally. At one point, Laura puts on her mother's old coat, which of course is a poor fit for her, an action symbolic of her vague efforts at imitating a personality so alien to her powers and her own nature. She knows that she is like the unicorn or the blue rose, wrong for real life. Laura cannot see that Amanda exaggerates this wrongness by her impossibly romantic dreams. When Laura entered her high-school classes late, the sound of the brace on her leg seemed to her like claps of thunder. She thinks her affliction is dreadful because Amanda thinks it is. This flaw, a symbol of the crippling of a sensitive person thrust into a world unwilling to make allowances for sensitivity, becomes the cause of her separation from reality.

For Tennessee Williams, his sister became a symbol of the sensitive and the outcast, for their sensitivity invariably subjects them to mutilation. It is no accident that Laura's story appears in the collection of early fiction, eventually published under the title *One Arm*. Every important character in the book—the college students, the vagrant poet, the sallow little masochist, the perverted artist, the consumptive factory worker, the one-armed male prostitute, and the girl with her glass menagerie, can be destroyed at a touch. All, like Laura, are crippled in some way. The radiance of such people is like a "piece of translucent glass touched by light, given a momentary radiance, not actual, not lasting."

Laura contrasts with the normal, middle-class, realistic Jim, with whom she falls dreamily in love. Their views show their complete diversity. For example, when they discuss her favorite animal, the unicorn, Laura thinks of him as intrinsically different from his companions, while Jim sees him simply as a horse with a horn. In the same way, Jim sees the defect in Laura's leg as only unfortunately incidental to her normal body, while Laura feels that the flaw transforms her whole being. Jim can sympathize with Laura's world of glass and candlelight for this evening, but his real interests are in the modern mechanical world of self-improvement. He is the only character in the play who goes out of the house into a normal world of "reality." Tom emphasizes this in the opening and closing lines of the play; he is an emissary from another world; he does not belong to the Wingfield world of dreams and fears and unexpressed desires.

Jim is not an especially effective character study because Williams can feel little sympathy with such a substantial and placid citizen. Yet he is a kindly reminder of the reasonable, normal human pattern, like the men Williams had met at the shoe factory—clean-living, honest, sweet-natured, materialistic, eager American businessmen. The gently satirical portrait bears no relationship to the later, bitter portraits of C. C. Williams.

Since it is characteristic of Amanda, more than of the others, to long for everything Jim represents, he is for her an archetype of the "long delayed but always expected something we live for." Unintentionally, Jim breaks up the Wingfield dreams. We suspect that his entrance into the household is part of a recurring pattern. Every contact with the real world has shattered Amanda's unrealistic hopes over the years.

The setting of *The Glass Menagerie* was interesting in its symbolism and technical experimentation. Moving from the deep South to St. Louis for his story, Williams retains the memory of the South, as a haunting presence under the superimposed Midwestern setting. The audience, never seeing the gracious mansion that was the scene of Amanda's girlhood, feels its remembered glory and its contrast to the mean present. Awareness of the past is always an element in Williams's plays. His characters live beyond the fleeting moments of the drama—back into a glowing past and shrinking from a terrifying future. For both Amanda and the later Blanche of *Streetcar*, the South forms an image of youth, love, purity, all of the ideals that have crumbled along with the mansions and the family fortunes.

Since the setting in *Menagerie* is that of a "memory play," Tennessee Williams could feel free in its staging. His theory of expressionism is propounded in the introductory production notes, which are, in fact, directly applied in the play. His concept of the "new, plastic theatre" was probably influenced by Erwin Piscator, a German director who had helped him at the New School Seminar. He suggests that in *The Glass Menagerie*'s "considerably delicate or tenuous material, atmospheric touches and subtleties of direction play a particularly important part." Williams justifies such unconventional techniques as expressionism or impressionism on the basis that their subjectivity provides a "closer approach to truth." No playwright should use such devices in an effort to avoid the "responsibility of dealing with reality, or interpreting experience." But he believes that the new drama has followed the other arts in recognizing that realism is not the key to reality.

"The straight realistic play with its genuine frigidaire and authentic ice-cubes, its characters that speak exactly as its audience speaks," he says, "corresponds to the academic landscape and has the same virtue of photographic likeness." Then, with unique optimism regarding current artistic tastes, he continues, "Everyone should know nowadays the unimportance of the photographic in art: that truth, life, or reality is an organic thing which the poetic imagination can represent or suggest, in essence, only through transformation, through changing into other forms than those which were merely present in appearance." The philosophy expressed here is in accord with the nineteenth-century Romantics and their followers in this century. The expressionistic concepts propounded in this preface have proved so effective in Tennessee Williams's work that set-designers have usually chosen to use expressionistic even when realistic settings are called for in Williams's manuscripts. Williams has a poet's weakness for symbols, and this modern technique frees his hand for scattering them about the stage. Their use to reflect, emphasize, and contrast with the meanings of the actions and the words has become a trademark of the Williams play.

The Glass Menagerie projected symbolic elements in line with Williams's newly enunciated theory. To reinforce the spoken word the author recommends the use of a screen device. A legend or image projected on the screen for the duration of the scene emphasizes the most important phrase. For example, in the scene where Jim remembers that Laura is the girl who was stricken with pleurosis, whom he mistakenly nicknamed "Blue Roses," the legend on the screen accents the peculiarity of the name, and the audience, along with Laura, is made more keenly aware that although blue is beautiful, it is wrong for roses. Eddie Dowling [the producer] considered this device superfluous and omitted it from the stage production, and wisely so. Mr. Gassner also considered the screen device "redundant and rather precious." Williams is "straining for effect not knowing that his simple tale, so hauntingly self-sufficient, needs no adornments."

Williams's expressionist theory also leads him to another variation from strictly realistic drama. The lighting changes with the mood. The stage is as dim as the participants' lives. Shafts of light flicker onto selected areas or actors, "sometimes in contradiction to what is the apparent center." When Tom and Amanda are quarreling, the light on them is low red, while Laura stands in a pool of light of that "peculiar pristine clarity such as light used in early religious portraits of saints or madonnas." The tone, strength, and occurrence of the lights have the power of emotional emphasis. In a technique reminiscent of Chekhov's, Williams heightens the emotional truths of the scenes and the reality of the internal action through unusual external effects.

The musical accompaniment of *The Glass Menagerie* is another element of Tennessee Williams's expressionism that characterizes his dramas. The theme is a tune called "The Glass Menagerie," composed by Paul Bowles. It is "like circus music, not when you are on the grounds or in the immediate vicinity of the parade, but when you are at some distance and very likely thinking of something else. . . . It expresses the surface vivacity of life and the underlying strain of immutable and inexpressible sorrow." The music becomes Laura's symbol of this world which is like a circus for her—heard from a safe distance—and of her retreat into a world of music as well as of glass.

The depiction of the Wingfields' apartment also follows the dicta of expressionism. The ugly uniformity of the tenements depresses Tom and makes him frantic to escape. The place is described as "one of those vast hive-like conglomerations of cellular living-units that flower as warty growths in overcrowded urban centers of lower middle-class populations." They are, says the temporarily socially conscious author, "symptomatic of the impulse of this largest and fundamentally enslaved section of American society to avoid fluidity and differentiation and to exist and function as one interfused mass of automatism." Of the characters in the play, only Tom seems aware of this grotesque uniformity; and since the whole story takes place in his memory, he would naturally exaggerate the dismal reality he sees.

On both sides of the building, dark, narrow alleys run into "murky canyons of tangled clotheslines, garbage cans and sinister lattice-work of neighboring fire escapes." The meaning of these alleys is clear if the reader recalls Tom's picture of "Death Valley," where cats were trapped and killed by a vicious dog. The predicament becomes a symbol of his factory work, murderous to his creative imagination. For Laura, the alley represents the ugly world from which she retreats to gaze into her tiny glass figures. For Amanda, too, the alley is the world of her present hopeless poverty and confusion from which she retreats into her make-believe world of memory and pretence. Inside the apartment, where she tries to create an illusion of gentility, her husband's portrait grins at her futile efforts.

The apartment is entered by a fire escape, "a structure whose name is a touch of accidental poetic truth, for all those huge buildings are always burning with the slow and implacable fires of human desperation." On this fire escape, Tom Wingfield seeks liberation from his private hell. It is no mere coincidence that this play's solution (like those of *Battle of Angels* and *Stairs to the Roof*) centers around the stairway. Stairs are the tangible sign of man's change in levels of reality.

It would seem that every item of the setting is symbolic—even the Paradise Dance Hall, across the alley. There sexual gratification provides the cliff-dwellers of the neighborhood a temporary paradise. In their moments of closeness, they achieve the escape that Tom finds in his movies and poetry.

The story, characterization, and setting of this play combine to form a "static" drama, a technique Williams has used in other plays, including the rewrite of *Battle of Angels*. Action is softened by this "patina" of time and distance; framed in memory, it becomes more artistic. The interest of this play depends on neither incident nor situation. Unlike most of Williams's other works, which are charged with sensationalism and sex, this story holds the audience by the revelation of quiet and ordinary truths. This play, unique among Williams's dramas, combines poetic and unrealistic techniques with grim naturalism to achieve a gossamer effect of compassion, fragility, and frustration, typical of Tennessee Williams at his most sensitive and natural best. The play is his most effective poetic work.

The Function of Gentlemen Callers: A Note on Tennessee Williams's *The Glass Menagerie*

Elmo Howell

In the stage directions for *Sweet Bird of Youth*, Tennessee Williams states that Chance Wayne, though an aging roué, has "the kind of body that white silk pajamas are, or ought to be, made for." To accompany the visual effects of the opening bedroom scene, a church bell tolls, and "from another church, nearer, a choir starts singing The Hallelujah Chorus." It is Easter Sunday morning in a decadent town in the deep South.

Williams's most striking effects are derived from the ambivalence produced by a Puritan conscience and a delight in shock, which even in his latest work retains the puckish innocence of a boy. Boss Finley lives behind white columns with his daughter named Heavenly; but his daughter is despoiled already, and Finley is a Southern demagogue whose henchmen close in at the last scene to castrate the figure in white pajamas. Matter and spirit—these are the opposites in Williams's world, though the opposition is more theatrical than real since spirit has long been conquered and, like the bells of Easter morning, serves only as a reminder of what has been lost.

Williams frequently uses the South in this equation as symbolic of an elusive grace—spiritual, if you will—uncommon in a technological society. His attitude is by no means consistent. More often than not, his Southern women are doxies or fallen ladies and his men

From *Notes on Mississippi Writers* 2, no. 3 (Winter 1970). © 1970 by *Notes on Mississippi Writers*.

the vulgar bullies of hillbilly origin like Boss Finley or Big Daddy of *Cat on a Hot Tin Roof.* But Williams enjoyed a great many years of childhood security in Mississippi, where he was born in the vicarage home of his grandfather in Columbus. Although he abhors Southern racism, he has an affinity with the aristocratic ideal, which he associates with the venerable figure of his grandfather, a gentleman of the old school and one of the strongest influences in his life.

Amanda Wingfield of *The Glass Menagerie*, a faded belle from Blue Mountain, Mississippi, with recollections of seventeen gentlemen callers in one afternoon, exults in her Southern past to make more bearable the St. Louis industrial slum where an unfortunate marriage has brought her. A garrulous and silly woman, she torments her son about his drinking and his movie-going and makes her daughter's life miserable because Laura, unable to cope with a physical infirmity and a natural shyness, seeks refuge in an imaginary world of a glass menagerie. Amanda's patter about the gentlemen callers begins as a tiresome joke; but in the course of the play by some obscure alchemy of which the author himself seems unaware, the Southern past confers on Amanda a tragic depth which her children do not share.

The Glass Menagerie is a product of Williams's own experience. When his family left Mississippi to live in St. Louis when he was about twelve, he remembered the rural South as "a wide spacious land that you can breathe in." Like Amanda, he prized his Southern associations. "My folks," he said, "were pioneer Tennesseans, mostly of a military and political disposition, some of them, such as Nollichucky Jack Sevier, having been famous Indian fighters when the South was being settled. I am also related to the late Senator John Sharp Williams, who was a famous silver-tongued orator of Mississippi." Above all, the quiet rectory life of his childhood in Columbus and then in Clarksdale (the Blue Mountain of his plays) is lodged in his memory and serves as a touchstone against which the tawdriness of urban life is measured. The moon over Garfinkel's delicatessen, the alley where cats fight and couples wander from the Paradise Dance Hall, the fire escape which reminds Amanda of her Southern verandah, the dark rooms where the sun never penetrates—all are painful images drawn from the stark contrast of two cultures.

Otto Reinert calls *The Glass Menagerie* a play "in the modern democratic tradition that assumes that serious drama can be made of the sufferings of small people." The play is indeed about small people. Tom Wingfield has his poetry and his dreams and eventually his escape, like his father. Laura is crippled, physically and emotionally. Amanda is stronger than either, but under the pressure of circumstance she also gives way to littleness, in her constant nagging and in impossible demands on her children. In what way, then, does the play rise above littleness? It is in Amanda Wingfield's memory, "seated predominantly in the heart," of her life before she came to an urban industrialized North, which Williams refers to as "the fundamentally enslaved section of American society." The tragic dimension of the play is centered in Amanda, for neither of her children is capable of seeing, as the mother sees, their starved present in the light of a larger past.

Amanda is an ordinary woman who is somehow transfigured by the memory of her early life in Mississippi and who tries to pass the influence on to her children. She exaggerates her glories, like the number of gentlemen callers, but the idea of a very different way of life is real, and this is enough to establish her as the dominant interest in the play. When she talks of Blue Mountain, her children patronize her and laugh behind her back. "I know what's coming," Tom says. "Yes. But let her tell it," Laura says. "She loves to tell it." And then Amanda simpers and capers in a mere burlesque of the high life she recalls as a Southern belle. Tom wants to know how she managed to entertain all those gentlemen callers. She knew the art of conversation, she says. A girl in those days needed more than a pretty face and figure, "although I wasn't slighted in either respect"; she had to know how to talk and to discuss significant things. "Never anything coarse or common or vulgar." Amanda's escape from the dreary present is different from Tom's and Laura's. They try to escape reality, but she in her own way is coming to grips with it, by trying to make a breadwinner out of Tom and by securing Laura's future with a career or marriage. "Both of my children—they're *unusual* children! Don't you think I know it? I'm so—proud!" The gentlemen callers are not designed to reflect her popularity so much as to suggest to her children the larger possibilities that life has to offer which they from limited experience are unable to see.

In spite of her silliness, the mother represents the fundamental decencies that Williams must have known in his Southern boyhood. She reacts with Victorian fervor when Tom brings home a book by D. H. Lawrence. "I cannot control the output of diseased minds and the people who cater to them, but I won't allow such filth brought into my house." When Tom mentions instinct, she picks up the word as if it were obscene. "It belongs properly to animals," she says; "Christians and adults have got away from it." She makes herself ridiculous in voicing the pruderies of the Bible Belt—that is the first impression of her; but as her character unfolds, her Puritan reservations, like her affected Southern manners, become part of a larger nature that commands respect. The closing scene of Amanda comforting her daughter after Tom has left them and Laura's hopes have failed elevates the mind in terms of the mother's suffering and her acceptance of it. "Her silliness is gone," says the author, "and she has dignity and tragic beauty."

In the figure of Amanda, Tennessee Williams uses his Southern background to enforce a unity of effect where theme is imprecisely imagined. Mother, son, and daughter are all personal with the author and their sufferings deeply felt, but no one of them has a certain preeminence in the author's mind. Only in the mother, as the story progresses, does a definite meaning emerge. The gentlemen callers begin as a joke; Amanda herself is a joke, in the eyes of her children and of the generation which they represent; but Williams's concept of a very different way of life in his native South enables him to transmute the silly mother and her dreams into something which is noble and true. In its larger meaning, Amanda's tragedy becomes a parable of the inadequacy of modern life.

The Glass Menagerie suggests the wholesome use of a living tradition to the artist. Unlike his fellow Mississippians William Faulkner and Eudora Welty, Williams has no strong feeling for place. Like Tom Wingfield, he is a rover; and when he returns to Mississippi for a setting it is more often than not for exotic effect, not for cultural reasons, as in *The Rose Tatoo*, where he peoples a Gulf Coast town with Sicilians. But the placid environs of his boyhood fixed in his imagination an ideal which in his best moments lifts his drama above mere sensation. "Whoever you are," says Blanche DuBois to the attendant from the state institution, "I have always depended on the kindness of strangers." In spite of her weakness, Blanche is the noblest creation of *Streetcar* and the source of the tension, for she, like Amanda, recalls for Williams a certain beneficence in human relations which has all but disappeared. Williams's use of the South for shock value is gross and deliberate, but the part the South plays in shaping his moral vision is more impressive because it is unselfconscious. In the character of Amanda, *The Glass Menagerie* moves almost imperceptibly into mythic meaning.

Tennessee Williams's Unicorn Broken Again

Gilbert Debusscher

A writer who undertakes to give literary shape to roughly identical material in different genres often draws a critical response that attempts to assess his success by measuring the various offerings against each other. The dramas of Tennessee Williams have repeatedly been approached through the short stories or the poems he uses as blueprints for his plays. No book-length study of Williams's work is without a description and an analysis, sometimes lengthily drawn out, of the successive developments through which his literary constructs acquire their final dramatic physiognomy and, more often than not, their most felicitous and successful expression. Moreover, a growing number of articles are devoted to this process of refining, by now characteristic of Williams's working method, which a critic once aptly described as a transmutation of sand into Baccarat crystal.

Of all the works in the canon, none have been more often scrutinized from this point of view than *The Glass Menagerie* and its companion piece "Portrait of a Girl in Glass." Only recently several critics have addressed themselves again to the successive versions in dramatic or nondramatic form of the Wingfields' story and have come up with fresh information and new insights.

In spite of this revived interest in Williams's first commercial success, a study that would compare and contrast, not theme and characters (they are basically the same in play and short story) but the

From *Revue Belge de Philologie et d'Histoire* 49 (1971). ©1971 by *Revue Belge de Philologie et d'Histoire*.

texts themselves, is still lacking. The title of Mr. Grigor Pavlov's essay "A Comparative Study of Tennessee Williams' *The Glass Menagerie* and 'Portrait of a Girl in Glass'" is likely therefore to arouse some interest; the introductory paragraph, however, defeats the expectations, for it states that "the aim of this paper is to analyse the short story 'Portrait of a Girl in Glass' and the play *The Glass Menagerie* by Tennessee Williams and to compare the manner in which he handles basically the same thematic material in two genres and the delineation of characters in the drama and the short story." In spite of this initial disappointment, anyone familiar enough with the ever-expanding bulk of Williams criticism would be ill-advised to stop there under the pretext that the following pages could only rehash old news. Indeed Mr. Pavlov treats his readers to considerations that differ notably and irritatingly from those one is led to expect after his introduction. It seems that the Bulgarian scholar loses sight, as early as the fourth paragraph, of his stated aims "to analyse" and "to compare" and attempts, instead, to *impose the view that the two works primarily chronicle the social dissolution of a typical lower-middle-class American family under strained material circumstances represented by the aftermath of the Great Depression.*

Two symptomatic sentences that give away Mr. Pavlov's real intentions stem the course of his exposé. His introduction leads to his key-thesis: "The main theme running both through play and short story is the disintegration of a petty bourgeois family." His concluding remarks are preceded by a quietly assured statement of similar import: "The process of the destruction of a middle class American family has been completed." The essay is shot through with twenty-six references to the "Great Economic Depression," the "American lower middle-class," the ruthless capitalist system that perverts people through its warped and jangled moral and ethical codes, the questionable literary tastes of the American bourgeois.

It is obvious that the critic is trying by means of ad nauseam repetition, to impose the view that *The Glass Menagerie* is a kind of dramatized social pamphlet, a play whose overall aim is to denounce, through the example of the Wingfields, the deplorable effects of capitalism.

Throughout his essay Mr. Pavlov casts the members of the Wingfield family as representatives of a social class. Thus he considers that what they experience is "the frustration, despair and confusion of the American lower class, left stunned and bleeding in the path of the economic tornado." Further he quotes the initial stage direction describing the Wingfield neighbourhood and states that it assumes the force of a generalization about the vast middle class of the United States, "this largest and fundamentally enslaved section of American society, suffocating in apartment buildings the color of dried blood and mustard!" Mr. Pavlov's premise raises the question of the Wingfields' representativity and, beyond that, of the importance and function of the social elements in the play.

Certainly, Amanda, a former Southern belle, Tom, "a poet with a job in a warehouse" and Laura, a morbidly shy "girl in glass," three eminently atypical characters, cannot be considered epitomes of a social class. There is no denying that the family's financial means (for all we know the $65 of Tom's monthly pay constitute their only regular income) put them within the revenue bracket of the lower middle class. Mr. Pavlov fails to point out, however, that none of the members of the trio are integrated to the social sphere in which they are forced to live. Williams scatters his play with hints that the Wingfields, far from epitomizing their milieu (as Arthur Miller's war manufacturer or salesman or immigrant worker do), refuse to accept their surroundings and are, in turn, rejected by the outside world. Amanda despises the Chinese laundry and Jewish delicatessen neighbourhood and rails against her stingy, speculating landlord; she has remained an active member of the D.A.R. organisation and the Acting Version introduces her with a vituperative speech against "Northern Episcopalians" who refused to give her a pew in the nearby church. Tom hates the "celotex interior! with fluorescent tubes!" of the factory; his workmates regard him with "suspicious hostility" because of his poetic activities; they consider him an outsider, "an oddly fashioned dog who trots across their path at some distance." Laura dislikes the music from the Paradise Dance Hall; her characterial shortcomings have kept people away from her: she has never managed to make friends in St. Louis. The Wingfields are then introduced less as representatives of the lower middle class than as aliens in it, less as "petty bourgeois" than as involuntary and sometimes infuriated exiles in a petty bourgeois milieu. Objectively they may be ranked with their urban ghetto neighbours; subjectively they are miles apart from them. And this spirit of "apartness" rather than a sense of belonging is what determines their actions in the play. Had Williams wanted primarily to comment on the lower middle class he would, no doubt, have selected less objectionable representatives.

There are indications in Mr. Pavlov's article that his misconception is based less on faulty reading than on deliberate distortion. To prove, against all evidence, that the "four characters are products of the Depression period," Mr. Pavlov quotes from the narrator's introductory speech. His comment on the description of the late thirties illustrates his characteristic method of twisting the work out of shape to fit his preconceived views:

> That was a time of profound social and political upheaval in the bourgeois world. *In Spain there was Guernica. Here there were disturbances of labor, in otherwise peaceful cities as Chicago, Cleveland, Saint Louis.*

Thus presented out of context, the narrator's comment seems to imply that the destruction of the Basque city, and more generally, the events in Spain are comparable in impact to the social unrest prevalent in American urban centres and would thus leave a profound mark on those experiencing them. Turning to the text of Tom's first words, the reader sees through Mr. Pavlov's tactics. The context in which the quoted passage appears runs as follows:

> In Spain there was revolution. Here there was only shouting and confusion. In Spain there was Guernica. Here there were disturbances of labour, sometimes pretty violent, in otherwise peaceful cities such as Chicago, Cleveland, Saint Louis. . . .
> This is the social background of the play. (*Music.*)

What Tom says, in effect, is then precisely the opposite of what Mr. Pavlov leads us to believe: compared to Spain, where World War II was in rehearsal, America witnessed only minor disturbances. The parallelism of construction of the two sentences invites the reader and spectator to extend the oppositive pattern established in the first on to the second. It is easy to see why Mr. Pavlov, wanting to emphasize the effect of the immediate social surroundings on the characters, would leave the first sentence out of his quotation. It is equally obvious that the concluding sentence of the passage would prove bothersome for someone trying to impose the view that *The Glass Menagerie* is a social picture. The last words of the narrator sound like the playwright's prophetic answer to Mr. Pavlov's contention. The few touches evoking "that quaint period the thirties" seem sufficient to Tom and, implicitly, to playwright Williams to call forth "the social background of the play" and to place the story of the Wingfields in the proper perspective. The place apportioned to these comments should be an objective measure of the playwright's interest in social problems and of their relevance to this play. In fact, social elements never acquire in Williams's works the prominence that Mr. Pavlov would ascribe to them. In this particular case, the playwright uses the context of the aftermath of the Great Depression as an intensifying factor of the personal conflicts, creating a sense of urgency which heightens the dramatic tensions. Mr. Pavlov points out quite rightly that "in the short story . . . there is no concrete reference to the social turbulence of the day, no mention is made of the economic chaos reigning without the gloomy Wingfield apartment." He further notices that Williams nevertheless introduces obliquely the atmosphere of the outside world, through his description of a narrow areaway called Death Valley and of the tragic end of cats cornered there by vicious chows. Mr. Pavlov thus unwittingly suggests what the Depression background in the play really amounts to, viz. a means to evoke a world in which man is trapped (not by social circumstances exclusively) like an alley cat pursued by a dog in a dead-end street.

It is then less the social picture in itself that Williams is interested in than the effect of strained circumstances on his characters, less middle-class America under financial stress than man in general reacting to adversity of any nature. As Joseph N. Riddel noticed in connection with another play: "To see *A Streetcar Named Desire* as a realistic slice-of-life is to mistake its ambitious theme; to find it social protest is to misread the surface, for just as in *The Glass Menagerie*, Williams gets in his social licks while groping for a more universal statement."

For having approached the play with preconceived views Mr. Pavlov has overlooked Williams's "more universal statement." Yet had he carefully carried through his initial project "to compare" the short story with the play, he might have noticed revelatory omissions or substitutions. Thus he might have been led to stress the disappearance from among the objects surrounding Laura in the short story of "a remarkably bad religious painting, a very effeminate head of Christ with teardrops visible just below the eyes" and the concomitant introduction of a unicorn in the play, among the figurines of the girl's glass collection.

This observation might have conceivably set him wondering whether the function of the sanctimonious painting (a sarcastic comment on religious values) had been transferred to the glass animal or whether Williams had simply dropped his Christian reference from the text of the play. Had Mr. Pavlov then been more familiar with Williams criticism he would certainly have remembered that in 1961, Signi Falk had noticed traces of Christian elements in *The Glass Menagerie* but had attributed them to the playwright's affected efforts to hoist the play to a more poetic level. Commenting on the crucial scene of Laura's interview with the gentleman caller, she stated in the sweet-sour manner characteristic of her whole book: "This scene is one of the best that Williams has written. It closes, however, on a symbolic and precious note, incongruous in spirit. The playwright mixes up romantic love and religion—as he was to do so often in later years—and he mixes his metaphors as well. He refers to Laura's face as an altar and speaks of the holy candles being snuffed out; he then describes the altar of her face as having a look of desolation. This is posturing, not poetry." These overtones of the scene in which the unicorn plays a central part are mentioned again in the concluding paragraph of Beaurline's article, which lists some further religious paraphernalia whose absence from the short story and introduction into the play escaped Mr. Pavlov's attention: "Williams' most successful revisions of stage directions unobtrusively change the story's matter-of-fact tone into memory. The narrator of the story becomes the presenter of the play, and significant stage properties appear in the big scene: the blasted candelabra from the altar of the Church of the Heavenly Rest, the ice cream, fruit punch, and macaroons. In the reading version the ice cream was replaced with dandelion wine (for a mock communion?), and Amanda 'baptizes' herself with lemonade—all of which contributes to the vague religious impression of the scene" (*The Glass Menagerie: From Story to Play*).

The religious elements which might well begin to emerge at this point as the essential difference between the short story and the play had been given extensive independent scrutiny by Roger B. Stein in 1964. Stein showed convincingly that in stage directions and dialogue throughout the play, religious overtones could be traced which are almost entirely absent from the short story. After commenting on the religious aura surrounding each of the Wingfields, Stein finally comes to Jim O'Connor, the gentleman caller:

> It remains therefore for Jim to come as the Savior to this
> Friday night supper. The air of expectancy is great with

the ritualistic dressing of Laura, the tension and the oppressive heat. Jim's arrival is marked by the coming of rain, but the hopes of fertility and renewal which this might suggest are soon dashed. . . . The failure of electric power after dinner—previsioning the blackout of the world—leads to Amanda's joking question, "Where was Moses when the lights went off?" This suggests another Savior who would lead his people from the desert into the promised land, but the answer to her question is "In the dark."

Jim's attempt to play the modern Savior is an abysmal failure. In the after-dinner scene, he offers Laura the sacrament—wine and "life-savers," in this case—and a Dale Carnegie version of the Sermon on the Mount—self-help rather than divine help—but to no avail.

However, the part played by the unicorn in the pattern of religious symbolism that pervades the play, and particularly in the symbolic characterization of Jim, escaped Stein's critical attention.

The peculiar glass figurine grows to prominence only in the last scene (scene 7) the interview scene between Laura and Jim. Thus far in the play, it had been only an undistinguished part of the glass menagerie, Laura's fragile refuge against the unbearable tension of the outside world. In the course of the interview the small animal comes to be connected with *both* Laura and Jim. This double association points to its twofold symbolic meaning.

When Laura designates the unicorn to Jim's attention as the figurine dearest to her, she also points to the horn on its forehead and admits that his singularity may make him feel lonesome and certainly makes him unfit for life in a world tending to reduce living creatures to "one interfused mass of automatism." Her warning to Jim "Oh, be careful—if you breathe, it breaks!" may well connote that it is only an imaginary creature, a mythic lie and that breathing, a basic manifestation of real life, might be too much of a test for it as it is, in a different sense, for her. The unicorn is thus perhaps more appropriately than the glass collection as a whole, a perfect symbol for Laura since, to the overtones of fragility and delicate beauty of all the glass figurines, it adds those of uniqueness and, as a consequence almost, of freakishness. Jim, however, is not captivated by Laura's fable about her animals. To draw her away from her morbid fascination and palliate the lack of conversation, he invites her to "cut the rug a little" at the sound of a waltz coming from the Paradise Dance Hall. Jim thus lures Laura out of the dreamlike universe of which the unicorn is the centre, away from her reverie and invites her to move with him towards the world of the alley, to become identical with the innumerable couples moving, indistinct in the flickering light of the "deceptive rainbows" or seeking the relative privacy of the areaway in search of a fleeting moment of sensual intimacy. As Jim swings Laura into motion, they hit the little table and the unicorn falls to the floor; his little horn is broken off his head. As a figurine epitomizing the glass menagerie, i.e., Laura's possibility of escaping into an unreal world of glass, and as a symbol of Laura herself, the unicorn breaks, aptly it would seem, at the moment when the girl emerges from the world of her lifeless companions and transfers the refuge overtones connected with it onto the person of Jim. The breaking of the unicorn marks the capital turning point in Laura's life when the flickering, immature world of glass toys loses its attractiveness in her eyes and she feels rising in her, the desire to disregard her freakishness, to dance like all the others, to belong to the world of the adults. The event symbolizes a kind of emotional defloration, the girl's irreversible loss of childlike innocence, the unavoidable mutilation that Williams sees as necessarily accompanying the process of growing up. Laura's reaction to the accident, however, reveals that she is less concerned about what she has lost than about what she vaguely senses might be a gain:

> LAURA: It doesn't matter, maybe it's a blessing in disguise.
> . . . It's no tragedy, Freckles. Glass breaks so easily.
> No matter how careful you are. The traffic jars the
> shelves and things fall off them. . . . I'll just imagine
> he had an operation. The horn was removed to make
> him feel less—freakish! (They both laugh.) Now he
> will feel more at home with the other horses, the
> ones that don't have horns.

Her surprisingly mild comment obliquely states her deep-seated desire to "feel more at home with the others." Excited at the perspective of being able to identify with the Paradise Dance Hall dwellers—she is "laughing breathlessly" a moment before the incident— Laura does not reproach Jim with clumsiness but, instead, indirectly expresses her gratitude for ending the era of the lonely freak. However, the expression of her gratitude is qualified by her equating of

Jim's effect on the unicorn with that of the heavy traffic outside. Jim is then obliquely identified with the hubbub outside and thus haloed with the destructive overtones always associated with trucks and lorries in Tennessee Williams's symbolic world. In this speech by Laura, Williams thus masterfully manages to maintain the ambiguous value of Jim at a crucial moment in the girl's life: a potential Saviour on the one hand, he is also her possible destroyer.

Now that he has charmed her away from her lifeless friends, Jim, the apprentice psychiatrist, imagines a shortcut that would miraculously make Laura come to real life:

> JIM: Somebody needs to build your confidence up and
> make you proud instead of shy and turning away
> and—blushing—somebody—ought to—ought to—
> kiss you Laura!

The new breath Jim wants to inspire Laura with is, in his opinion, that which will make her capable of living in his world. However, the warning of Laura about her favourite glass animal—"Oh, be careful—if you breathe, it breaks!" is still ringing in the play as Jim draws Laura to him and "kisses her on the lips."

The revelation of the world of physical intimacy unleashes in Laura a store of hidden feelings whose intensity is conveyed through her changing expression and prolonged silence: as he releases her, "she sinks on the sofa with a bright, dazed look"; after a moment, when he addresses her, "she looks up, smiling, not hearing the question"; as he offers her a piece of candy "she doesn't seem to hear him but her look grows brighter even."

Only when he proceeds through his revelations about the existence of a fiancée, rhapsodizing insensitively about "the power of love," does Laura's blissful look disappear. As the cruel revelation dawns upon her that after taking her away from her enchanted sphere, Jim cannot take her any further into the world of crude reality, Laura is literally thrown off balance by the violent contrast between her expectations and her experience: "Laura sways slightly forward and grips the arm of the sofa. . . . Leaning stiffly forward, clutching the arm of the sofa, Laura struggles visibly with her storm." At the end of Jim's rapturous evocation, the illumination of his passage in Laura's life is completely gone: "The holy candles in the altar of Laura's face have been snuffed out. There is a look of almost infinite desolation."

After a pause of crushing despair, Laura "opens her hand again on the broken glass ornament. Then she gently takes his hand and raises it level with her own. She carefully places the unicorn in the palm of his hand, then pushes his fingers closed upon it."

What Jim thus takes with him is the symbol of Laura's short-lived hopes, a souvenir of the normal girl he aroused in her for too brief a moment. Giving up the broken unicorn, Laura obliquely gives up all hope of ever being the normal girl it now represents, all desire of ever realising in the outside world the deeper yearnings Jim has laid bare in her. Immediately after surrendering the mutilated glass figurine, Laura retreats to the only refuge still available: "She rises unsteadily and crouches beside the victrola to wind it up." This slight motion underlines Laura's renunciation of the world; it makes clear, as Nelson noticed, that "she will never allow a Jim O'Connor to happen to her again."

Turning then to the connection of Jim with the unicorn, it is important to remember first of all that although Christian allusions are not absent from the short story, they are by no means as numerous there as in the play. The many Christian touches which Stein's article exhaustively pointed out were thus introduced when Williams was in the process of transforming the short story into the play. That is also when the unicorn is introduced as a prominent figure of the collection of glass animals. It is thus legitimate, from the outset, to consider that it too belongs to the elements of the Christian pattern.

Moreover, disregarding for a moment the texts themselves, we may recall that the unicorn is a traditional, time-honoured Christian symbol, usually representing purity. It is a frequent subject of Christian iconography and is often represented leading the cohort of pure animals as opposed to the serpent, leader of the impure animals. The first fathers of the Church sometimes equate it with Christ himself and the Annunciation is sometimes graphically represented by a unicorn leaping into Mary's womb.

In the light of this traditional symbolism, Jim's instrumental role in the disfigurement of the unicorn is obviously a decisive denial of his Messiah overtones. What he ultimately takes with him is as much a souvenir of Laura as the broken emblem of the Saviour which he now becomes identified with.

For Laura, the unicorn breaks, symptomatically, as the tinsel Paradise across the alley is haloed with deceptive "Salvation" overtones (the deceptive rainbows?). When those fade away with Jim's hasty departure, Laura is left with a void, an emptiness, a darkness.

Far from being the Saviour in Laura's life, Jim is an ugly caricature of it; instead of illuminating her life with a message of love, he leaves her in the dark. The fragile girl in glass is irremediably shattered for having mistaken a callous representative of the outside world for her Messiah.

The blackout at the end of the play underlines this thoroughly pessimistic outcome. It announces the blackout of war which is about to envelop the world of the late 1930s. It is also, as Stein notices, "the denial of any 'Rise and Shine' for these frail creatures. The church has been struck by lightning (and, we would add, the symbol of the Saviour broken) and all hope of resurrection has been lost in this damned universe where belief turns into metaphor, where man seems abandoned by his God, and where the echoes of prayer are heard only in blasphemy or irony. The bleakness of Williams's vision in *The Glass Menagerie* is complete."

Under the surface of the social melodrama that Mr. Pavlov sees in *The Glass Menagerie* thus lurks a play which reaches beyond the historical circumstances of the late 1930s and the national context in which it is set. It reveals a playwright whose interest in and depiction of social realities has never been more than occasional but whose metaphysical preoccupations, revealed as early as *Battle of Angels* (1940), have claimed a steadily increasing place in his work. Mr. Pavlov's partial emphasis might have been illuminating if he had simultaneously provided a stimulating insight into the play's full complexity by relating the aspect he has chosen to emphasize to the totality of the play. *The Glass Menagerie* as "a social melodrama" simply does not exist. Williams's *The Glass Menagerie* is another play, touching the position of man in a complex universe and the tensions engendered by this existential predicament. It is so controlled that it does not admit a division between a merely social and a metaphysical response. For having failed to recognize that *The Glass Menagerie* was as "considerably delicate or tenuous" in its balanced beauty as the little unicorn on its shelf, Mr. Pavlov turned into a new Jim O'Connor. In the disfigured work that emerges from his attempt "to analyse" and "to compare," it is impossible to recognize Williams's atmospheric, minor masterpiece.

Tennessee Williams, Theatre Poet in Prose

Frank Durham

Modern American attempts at verse drama have, on the whole, produced a harvest of respectable failures—*vide* the ambitious but incon-
gruously rhetorical and ornate plays of Maxwell Anderson and the
mannered and rather coldly calculated pieces by T. S. Eliot. Anderson bravely called for a return to poetry in the theatre and ground out
a kind of blank verse that wore the label "Poetry"—in red paint;
while Eliot, likewise, wrote on the need for poetry in drama but
staunchly maintained that the verse of the poet-dramatist should be
so subtly disguised as, for the most part, not to sound like verse at
all. One of the difficulties regarding the use of verse in the modern
theatre, as Eliot and [Archibald] MacLeish point out, is the belief that
the audience demands to see life as it is and that to such an audience
poetry (or is it merely verse?) sounds "artificial." Eliot does say that
there is a "peculiar range of sensibility [which] can be expressed by
dramatic poetry, at its moments of greatest intensity," "a fringe of
indefinite extent," beyond the capabilities of prose drama to express.
However, it is the contention of this [essay] that, while American
drama has increasingly sought to portray this "peculiar range of sensibility," the most successful means of doing so has not been verse. It
has, instead, been best portrayed by a new, or seemingly new, poetic
drama which eschews verse for an eclectic but organic union of both
verbal and nonverbal elements of the theatre, which many critics

From *South Atlantic Bulletin* 36, no. 2 (March 1971). ©1971 by South Atlantic Modern Language Association.

have recognized and which Tennessee Williams, one of its major practitioners, calls "plastic theatre." *The Glass Menagerie* will serve as a prime example of the form.

It is, of course, no longer necessary to argue that verse need not be metrical, but certainly the comparative failures of both Anderson and Eliot can be attributed largely to their clinging to the idea that metre is an essential of poetic drama. In fact, Anderson employed a somewhat modified blank verse, which in itself throws up a barrier between the contemporary play and the contemporary audience's acceptance of it; for blank verse is firmly fixed in the theatre-going mind with Shakespeare and the raft of pallid pseudo-Shakespeareans. To use it on stage today is somewhat analogous to employing the Dickensian chronicle for a modern psychological novel. It reeks of the past—and of fustian. And Eliot's adherence to a three-stressed line with a caesura is somewhat reminiscent of Anglo-Saxon verse.

What we have developed in twentieth-century America is a type of poetic drama peculiarly relevant to our own time, a drama which maintains a speaking acquaintance with surface reality but which, through all the means at its disposal, probes into and bodies forth what Eliot calls that "peculiar range of sensibility," the inner truth, the often unutterable essences of human action and human emotion. As Alan Downer says:

> Thus the true poet of the theater is not necessarily concerned in the least with the traditional forms and language of poetry, but with making all the elements at his disposal—plot, actor, action, stage, lighting, setting, music, speech—unite to serve as a vehicle for his theme, his vision, or his interpretation of man's fate.

And again:

> Properly handled, organically related to the action and purpose of the whole work, the devices of expressionism have permitted playwrights to penetrate beneath the surface of their situations, to reveal truths which realism by its nature tends to disguise. This penetration, this revelation of inner truth, brings the contemporary drama once more into a close relationship with the great repertory of the poetic drama of the past.
>
> (*Fifty Years of American Drama, 1900–1950*)

O'Neill was one of the first American playwrights to move thus beyond realism toward a new poetry of the theatre, but today its chief figure is Tennessee Williams.

In his "Author's Production Notes" to *The Glass Menagerie*, in which he discusses at length such "extra-literary" elements as music and lighting, Williams makes clear that he is consciously striving to write this new type of poetic drama. Calling the piece "a memory play" and saying that it is therefore to be produced "with unusual freedom of convention," he says:

> Because of its considerably delicate or tenuous material, atmospheric touches and subtleties of direction play a particularly important part. Expressionism and all other unconventional techniques in drama have only one valid aim, and that is a closer approach to truth. When a play employs unconventional techniques, it is not, or certainly shouldn't be, trying to escape its responsibility of dealing with reality, or interpreting experience, but is actually or should be attempting to find a closer approach, a more penetrating and vivid expression of things as they are. The straight realistic play with its genuine frigidaire and authentic ice-cubes, its characters that speak exactly as its audience speaks, corresponds to the academic landscape and has the same virtue of photographic likeness. Everyone should know nowadays the unimportance of the photographic in art: that truth, life, or reality is an organic thing which the poetic imagination can represent or suggest, in essence, only through transformation, through changing into other forms than those which merely present an appearance.
>
> These remarks are not meant as a preface only to this particular play. They have to do with a conception of a new, plastic theatre which must take the place of the exhausted theatre of realistic conventions if the theatre is to resume vitality as a part of our culture.
> (*The Glass Menagerie, A Play in Two Acts.* Acting Edition)

Thus Williams is consciously ushering in a new period in drama and a form, as Esther Merle Jackson says, distinctively and consciously American, a popular art form embodying all levels of American culture and life and in its intentions definitely poetic: "The search for a concrete expressive form—a shape congruent with poetic vision—is a motif that appears throughout the work of Williams" (*The Broken World of Tennessee Williams*).

His realization of the need for "transformation" suggests Frost's idea: "It is the height of poetry, the height of all thinking, the height of all poetic thinking, that attempts to say matter in terms of spirit and spirit in terms of matter." And, Frost continues, poetry (and thinking) is simply "saying one thing in terms of another." Elsewhere Frost maintains that "every poem is a new metaphor inside or it is nothing," and every poem is a symbol. Certainly in *The Glass Menagerie*, often called a "lyric play," Williams is employing this concept of "transformation," of the dominant metaphor and symbol. Tom, his narrator-character, begins by telling us: "I give you truth in the pleasant guise of illusion."

In *The Glass Menagerie* there are two dominant metaphors or symbols. The more obvious is, of course, glass, as the title itself implies. Laura's glass animals, especially the unicorn, which is broken, symbolize the tenuousness of her hold on reality, the ease with which her illusion may be shattered. Of her, Williams says, "the lovely fragility of glass which is her image." This symbol is relevant to the other characters also, for their ability to exist at all in the world rests on illusions as easily destroyed as the unicorn. Without her belief in her romantic past and in Laura's ultimate wooing by the nonexistent gentleman caller, Amanda, who is the strongest, would be unable to face the harsh struggle for survival, would lose that fierce strength which in her is both comic and tragically admirable. At the touch of truth, her world will shatter into a thousand irretrievable fragments. The gentleman caller, Jim O'Connor, is also sustained by two illusions, that of his great success and promise in high school and that of his future triumph based on the empty slogans of his television night course: "Because I believe in the future of television! I want to be ready to go right up along with it. . . . I'm planning to get in on the ground floor. Oh, I've already made the right connections. All that remains now is for the industry itself to get under way—full steam! You know, *knowledge*—Zzzzppp! *Money*—Zzzzzzpp! POWER! Wham! That's the cycle democracy is built on!" Jim himself, as Tom tells us, is the momentary and disappointing embodiment of Laura and Amanda's illusion—"But having a poet's weakness for symbols, I am using this character as a symbol— as the long-delayed but always expected something we live for." Tom, despising his job in the warehouse, escaping temporarily into the fantasy world of the movies, cherishes the ideal of the absconded father ("He was a telephone man who fell in love with long distance.") and envies Malvolio the Magician, who, nailed inside a coffin, "got out without removing one nail." But in Tom's case glass is both fragile and everlasting, for his physical escape brings no real liberation. Though he travels widely, the trap still holds him:

> Perhaps it was a familiar bit of music. Perhaps it was only a piece of transparent glass. . . . Perhaps I am walking along a street at night, in some strange city, before I have found companions, and I pass the lighted window of a shop where perfume is sold. The window is filled with pieces of colored glass, tiny transparent bottles in delicate colors, like bits of a shattered rainbow. Then all at once my sister touches my shoulder. I turn around and look into her eyes.

While glass is the more obvious of the metaphors or symbols which govern the play—and it is, to me, the symbol of the theme—the motion picture serves as the symbol determining the overall form of the play. Tom, the narrator, through whose consciousness we see the entire action, tells us at the start, "The play is memory. . . . Being a memory play, it is dimly lighted, it is sentimental, it is not realistic." Since it is Tom's memory and since Tom's escape from reality is the motion picture, Williams logically portrays Tom's memories in terms of the motion picture, the silent film even though dialogue is used. The structure and rhythmic flow of the scenes are like those of the motion picture. The screen device, generally omitted in production, resembles closely the use of subtitles on the silent screen, and Williams even employs simulated close-ups on several occasions, focusing his spotlight on individuals or objects, such as the father's photograph, much in the manner of the camera.

Once Tom's initial address to the audience establishes the entire play as memory, the action begins. The opening scene, that of Amanda and Laura in the dining room at the rear of the living room, commences as if it were what in motion pictures is called a long shot, for the two women are seen through a pair of scrim curtains which achieve the effect of both unreality and distance. First, the scrim representing the outside wall is raised, and Tom joins the women. Then Williams calls for the raising of the inner scrim, and the whole effect is like that of a camera dollying in for a closer shot. In the most widely published version, though not in the Acting Edition, Williams calls for subtitles and images to be projected "on a section of wall between the front-room and the dining-room," like those of the silent film. In such films a subtitle was often used at the beginning of a scene to tell the audience what to expect, sometimes to give the mood or thematic significance of the images to follow. When Laura and Amanda are revealed the subtitle is "OÙ SONT LES NEIGES." Williams says that the screen device was originally intended

> to give accent to certain values in each scene. Each scene contains a particular point (or several) which is structurally most important. In an episodic play, such as this, the basic structure or narrative line may be obscured from the audience; the effect may seem fragmentary rather than architectural. . . . The legend or image upon the screen will strengthen the effect of what is merely allusion in the writing and allow the primary point to be made more simply and lightly than if the entire responsibility were on the spoken lines.

In short, Williams is describing a structure remarkably close to that of the silent film— a series of short scenes, each making one or more points, with little or no transition between. The cumulative effect of these scenes, the relationships achieved by their juxtaposition and flow—these resemble what is in film called montage, originally associated with the work of Griffith and Eisenstein. Several critics have likened Williams's technique to that of the cinema and have used the term *montage* in their analyses of his structure.

In his comments on lighting and in his use of it in the play, Williams frequently suggests cinematic camera shots. He employs light, for example, for reaction close-ups. He says,

> Shafts of light are focused on selected areas or actors, sometimes in contradistinction to what is the apparent center. For instance, in the quarrel scene between Tom and Amanda, in which Laura has no active part, the clearest pool of light is on her figure. This is also true of the supper scene, when her silent figure on the sofa should remain the visual center.

In this way, the emphasis is not on the action itself but on a character's reaction to that action, the character highlighted as if in a close-up. And somewhat reminiscent of the diffused lighting Griffith used to employ to heighten the fragility of the young Lillian Gish or Mae Marsh, Williams calls for a special lighting of Laura: "The light upon Laura should be distinct from the others, having a peculiar pristine clarity such as the light used in early religious portraits of female saints or madonnas." He further says that throughout the production the light should suggest that in religious art, notably the work of El Greco, and that such lighting will make the use of the screen device more effective. The highlighting of the father's photograph has already been cited, and yet another outstanding example of the use of the cinematic close-up comes in act 1, scene 3, when Amanda tries to sell magazine subscriptions on the telephone. The light in the alley where Tom is fades out, *"and a head-spot falls on* AMANDA, *at phone in living-room."* The rest of the stage is dark, and Amanda stands alone in a circle of light revealing only her face. At the conclusion of her scene, *"Dining-room and living-room lights dim in. Reading lamp lights up at the same time."* The close-up gives way to a longer shot of the whole room. Speaking generally of the lighting, Williams says: "A free, imaginative use of light can be of enormous value in giving a mobile, plastic quality to plays of a more or less static nature."

In the motion picture, both silent and sound, music has been a key element. For silent films whole scores were sometimes composed, for example, that were played by the full orchestra which accompanied the initial road-showing of *The Big Parade* and *Ben Hur;* and for lesser films there was usually a music cue-sheet to guide the organist or pianist in his underlining of the mood or action of various scenes. Throughout the Acting Edition of *The Glass Menagerie* there are many music cues, and Williams stresses the importance of music as an "extra-literary accent" in the production. He calls for a "single recurring tune, 'The Glass Menagerie,'" to supply "emotional emphasis to suitable passages," and the mood of memory is established at the outset by *"dance-hall music. . . . Old popular music of, say, 1915–1920 period."* The music, in general, is dim, like music far away. "It seems . . . to continue almost interminably and it weaves in and out of your preoccupied consciousness." It should be both gay and sad, expressing the beauty and the fragility of glass. "Both of these ideas should be woven into the recurring tune, which dips in and out of the play as if it were carried on wind that changes." It serves, too, as a link between the narrator and his story and helps to join the episodic, cinematic scenes: "Between each episode it returns as reference to the emotion, nostalgia, which is the condition of the play. It is primarily Laura's music and therefore comes out most clearly when the play focuses upon her and the lovely fragility of glass which is her image." Thus, as in the film, music is employed for both mood and transition, evoking the atmosphere of memory and establishing relationships between the individual scenes, stressing the fluidity of the progress of an otherwise static plot. It is significant that the first dramatic version of the story Williams did was a motion picture script for Metro-Goldwyn-Mayer.

Other elements of the new non-verse poetic drama are also integral parts of the play. One of the most commented upon in the work of Williams is the symbol. In his preface to *Camino Real* Williams writes:

> I can't deny that I use a lot of those things called symbols, but being a self-defensive creature, I say that symbols are nothing but the natural speech of drama.
>
> We all have in our conscious and unconscious minds a great vocabulary of images, and I think all human communication is based on these images as are our dreams; and a symbol in a play has only one legitimate purpose, which is to say a thing more directly and simply and beautifully than it could be said in words.

Sometimes, it is true, Williams tends to overwhelm us with symbols, apparently for their own sake, but in *The Glass Menagerie* the symbols are employed effectively as organic elements in his poetic concept. A simple listing of them would include such obvious ones as the Paradise Dance Hall, the fire escape, the father's photograph, "Blue Roses," the idea of the gentleman caller, and many others. But the one most often discussed is the glass unicorn from Laura's little menagerie. Williams's use of it reveals him at his poetic best, for the unicorn not only stands for something else (or for several something elses) but is used dramatically to symbolize a change in relationships between two of the characters. Generally, the glass menagerie, including the unicorn, portrays Laura, her fragility, her delicacy, her beauty, her unworldliness, and at the same time the unicorn in particular symbolizes her life-maintaining illusion, her idealized concept of Jim, the high-school hero. When Jim appears in person, and the audience sees him as a sadly commonplace and frustrated human being, Laura still retains her illusions about him. But when she entrusts the unicorn in his hands, she says, "Oh, be careful—if you breathe, it breaks!" And Jim says, "Unicorns, aren't they extinct in the modern world?" Then in the ecstasy of the dance he knocks the unicorn from the table and it breaks—loses its horn, the thing that made it different from the others. And Laura, foreshadowing her coming disillusionment with the discovery of Jim's engagement, says, "The horn was removed to make him feel less—freakish! . . . Now he will feel more at home with the other horses, the ones who don't have horns." Thus Jim, the unicorn, the unique hero, subsides into the normal, the ordinary, himself destroying the aura of distinctiveness which Laura gave him, destroying her illusion—and yet she seems to accept this catastrophe with resignation. The unicorn has vanished, yes; but she still has her glass menagerie and the escape offered by her ancient phonograph records. One illusion is gone, but her other means of escape, her other illusions, still offer protection from life's harsh realities. Here the use of the symbol is not static but dynamic, embodying and underlining a major alteration in relationships.

While Eliot clung to the idea that poetic drama should be in verse, his concept of the effect which dramatic verse should create is relevant to Williams's use of language. Eliot says that audiences at a poetic, to him verse, drama

> expect poetry to be in rhythms which have lost touch with colloquial speech. What we have to do is to bring poetry into the world in which the audience lives and to which it returns when it leaves the theatre; not to transport the audience into some imaginary world totally unlike its own, an unreal world in which poetry is tolerated. What I should hope might be achieved, by a generation of dramatists having the benefit of our experience, is that the audience should find, at the moment of awareness that it is hearing poetry, that it is saying to itself: "*I could talk poetry too!*" Then we should not be transported into an artificial world; on the contrary, our own sordid, dreary daily world would be suddenly illuminated and transfigured.
>
> ("Poetry and Drama" in *On Poetry and Poets*)

It is just this, I believe, that Williams is able to accomplish and to do so without resorting to the dangerous artificialities of verse. He takes colloquial speech, often the colloquial speech of the South, and through a keen ear for its rhythms and patterns, its imagery and symbolism, lifts it to the level of poetry. It is *real* speech, but real speech intensified and heightened so that it not only evokes the pleasure of recognition but communicates the inexpressible, the very essence of character, emotion, and situation in a way traditionally associated with poetry.

The Glass Menagerie is filled with such passages, expressing a broad spectrum of the emotions—Tom's hilariously pathetic parodies of motion pictures and stage shows, Amanda's tragicomic magazine sales talk, and many others. The oft-cited jonquil speech is perhaps the best known. It has the patterned construction of a poem, its rhythms capture the emotions of its speaker, it embodies the comic-pathetic ideal of the gracious past, and it relies on floral imagery to enhance its resonance as poetry. Awaiting the arrival of the gentleman caller, Amanda dresses herself in the old gown of her youthful triumphs in the lost Never-Never Land of the Delta:

> This is the dress in which I led the cotillion. Won the cakewalk twice at Sunset Hill, wore one spring to the Governor's ball in Jackson!
>
> See how I sashayed around the ballroom, Laura?
>
> (*She raises her skirt and does a mincing step around the room.*)
>
> I wore it on Sundays for my gentlemen callers! I had it on the day I met your father—
>
> I had malaria fever all that spring. The change of climate from East Tennessee to the Delta—weakened resistance—I had a little temperature all the time—not enough to be serious—just enough to make me restless and giddy!—Invitations poured in—parties all over the Delta!—"Stay in bed," said Mother, "you have fever!"—but I just wouldn't.—I took quinine but kept on going, going!—Evenings, dances!—Afternoons, long, long rides! Picnics—lovely!—So lovely, that country in May.—All lacy with dogwood, literally flooded with jonquils!—That was the spring I had the craze for jonquils. Jonquils became an absolute obsession. Mother said, "Honey, there's no more room for jonquils." And still I kept on bringing in more jonquils. Whenever, wherever I saw them, I'd say, "Stop! Stop! I see jonquils!" I made the young men help me gather the jonquils! It was a joke, Amanda and her jon-

quils! Finally there were no more vases to hold them, every available space was filled with jonquils! No vases to hold them? All right, I'll hold them myself! And then I— (*She stops in front of the picture.* MUSIC) met your father!
Malaria fever and jonquils and then—this—boy.

Tom's final speech is another "set-piece," with its rhythmic flow, its recurrent imagery, its colloquial tone heightened by both the freight of the emotion and the suggestion of a pattern.

It is not only in the somewhat extended speeches that the poetic qualities are evident; many of the dialogues are made up of brief exchanges with the repetitive rhythmic patterns, almost like refrains, of verse but avoiding the rigidity of metre. Tom's teasing announcement of the visit of the gentleman caller is an example:

TOM: We are going to have one.
AMANDA: *What?*
TOM: A gentleman caller!
AMANDA: You mean you have asked some nice young
      man to come over? . . .
TOM: I've asked him to dinner.
AMANDA: You really did?
TOM: I did.
AMANDA: And did he—accept?
TOM: He did!
AMANDA: He did?
TOM: He did.
AMANDA: Well, isn't that lovely!
TOM: I thought you would be pleased.
AMANDA: It's definite, then?
TOM: Oh, very definite.
AMANDA: How soon?
TOM: Pretty soon.
AMANDA: How soon?
TOM: Very, very soon.

Here is approximately the give-and-take of traditional stichomythia retaining the quality of colloquialism.

Basic to the poetic qualities of Williams's language is his Southern origin, as several critics have noted. Marion Migid speaks of his

long line, which achieves its most striking effects through a Steinian repetitiveness, through the use of unexpected archaisms, and the insertion of unexpected "literary" words and ironically elegant turns of phrase. It is a stylized rendering of Southern diction, which is more self-conscious, more evasive, but also more imaginative than Northern speech.

("The Innocence of Tennessee Williams" in *Essays in the Modern Drama*)

Miss Jackson repeats this idea, stressing the fact that the natural symbolism of Southern diction has produced "a highly developed iconography." "This Southern aesthetic," she says, "has provided for the drama of Williams a kind of basic linguistic structure comparable to that which appeared in elementary stages of Greek tragedy."

Modern studies of poetry have frequently developed the concept of the poet as a user of myth and a creator of new myths. Certainly in other plays, notably *Orpheus Descending, Suddenly Last Summer,* and *Camino Real,* underlying the action and characters are classical myths and pagan rituals. In his later plays especially, as Miss Jackson points out, Williams "has put together a kind of modern myth, a symbolic representation of the life of man in our time." She sees this myth as "synthetic," "composed, after the manner of cinematic montage, from the fragments of many ethical, philosophical, social, poetic, intellectual, and religious perspectives . . . the image of modern man caught between opposing logics—man in search of a means of reconciliation." In *The Glass Menagerie* Williams reaches out tentatively for the materials of this myth. Basic to it is the idea of man's alienation from the world around him, man still clinging to old values in an environment where they are no longer relevant. Certain archetypal Williams figures begin to take shape in the play: the poet-wanderer, later to acquire sexual elements from D. H. Lawrence; the fragile girl threatened with destruction and either escaping into a dream world of the past or being corrupted by the jungle world of the present; the same girl in maturity, strong and defensive in her struggle against the present but finding sustenance through cherishing the ideal of lost grace and beauty. It is the myth of the alienated, the lost, seeking some sort of tenable posture in the present chaos. It is the source of the poet's vision. Williams himself says, "Personal lyricism is the outcry of prisoner to prisoner from the cell in solitary where each is confined for the duration of his life."

One of the constants of lyric poetry, and of much other poetry as well, is its immediacy, its capturing of the moment, the intense moment of experience and insight. Man is in constant battle with Time the Destroyer, and poetry is one of his oldest means of achieving victory. In his use of time and in his attitude toward it, Williams is typically the poet. He says, "Snatching the eternal out of the desperately fleeting is the great magic of human existence." In most of his plays his characters fight against time, its attrition and its ravages, and time becomes a major symbol of the adversary, malignant and malevolent. Amanda and Laura seek to turn time back, to recapture a past which they have perhaps idealized out of all semblance to reality but the very search for which gives meaning to their lives. On the other hand, Tom looks forward, toward a future time as an escape, but when that future becomes his present, he finds himself a prisoner of the past.

In *The Glass Menagerie* time is used another way, an equally poetic one. Tom stands with us in the immediate present. At the start he wears a merchant seaman's outfit indicative of escape from the physical past, of his having left his mother and sister behind. But through his consciousness we are carried back in time to his life in the drab apartment before his escape, and we retrace with him events leading to his decision to leave. Within this train of memory there are two types of time, the generalized and the specific, and through the use of these two we are given a deeper insight into the lives and relationships of the Wingfields. The first scene in the apartment, the dinner scene, is an example of generalized time. It is not any one particular dinner but a kind of abstraction of all the dinners shared by the trio in their life of entrapment. Amanda's admonitory speeches are ones often repeated, her stories of the seventeen gentlemen callers are oft-told tales—and Tom's irritated responses are those he makes each and every time the stories are retold. Amanda's telephone call to Ida Scott, with its pathetic attempts at salesmanship, is not one specific call, but, as the isolating spotlight tells us, it is an action out of time and place, the essence of a repeated action rather than a unique event. There are also unique moments in the parade of Tom's memory, highlights with a significance of their own—the imaginative reconstruction of the visit of Jim (for Tom was not present during some of the dialogue with Laura), for example. Through this multiple use of time Williams embodies both the concrete, the particular, and the general, the typical, his images often achieving the force of what Eliot has called the objective correlative of abstract truth.

From one point of view, as in *Death of a Salesman, The Glass Menagerie* actually transfixes and holds up for insight a single, brief moment of Tom's consciousness, a moment in the present in which, like Proust, he recapitulates the past, a past inextricably intertwined with the present and the future, freezes this moment—the intense moment of poetic insight, of lyric intuition. And this is often what a poem does. Williams is himself well aware of what he is doing. He says:

> It is this continual rush of time, so violent that it appears to be screaming, that deprives our actual lives of so much dignity and meaning, and it is, perhaps more than anything else, the *arrest of time* which has taken place in a completed work of art that gives certain plays their feeling of depth and significance. . . . If the world of the play did not offer us this occasion to view its characters under that special condition of a *world without time,* then, indeed, the characters and occurrences of drama would become equally pointless, equally trivial, as corresponding meetings and happenings in life.

In such a timeless world, like that of Greek tragedy, man becomes aware of his potential nobility:

> The audience can sit back in a comforting dusk to watch a world which is flooded with light and in which emotion and action have a dimension and dignity that they would likewise have in real existence, if only the shattering intrusion of time could be locked out.
>   ("The Timeless World of a Play" in *Perspectives on Drama*)

By arresting time, by embodying in a single moment the past, the present, and the future, by making this frozen moment one of tremendous intensity permitting an insight otherwise impossible, Williams has made *The Glass Menagerie* a lyric drama.

In conclusion, by utilizing many of the elements of poetry and the nonverbal facilities of the theatre—controlling metaphors and symbols, "transformation," lighting, music, movement, patterned colloquial speech, mythic elements, and the arresting of time to permit insight into the particular and the general—and by organically shaping these through a poet's vision—Williams in *The Glass Menagerie* exemplifies twentieth-century American poetic drama, free of the anachronism of verse, a poetic drama peculiarly adapted to the complexities of the present. Linking Williams with Arthur Miller, Kenneth Tynan says that both men, "committed to prose drama . . . have uncovered riches which make the English 'poetic revival' (of Eliot and Fry, for example) seem hollow, retrogressive, and—to use Cyril Connolly's coinage—praeterist."

The Revision of
The Glass Menagerie:
The Passing of Good Manners

Charles S. Watson

Tennessee Williams has frequently revised and published different texts of his plays. Two well-known examples are *Orpheus Descending* and *Cat on a Hot Tin Roof.* An especially interesting case is *The Glass Menagerie,* which exists in two published texts, the Library Edition and the later Acting Edition. The most noticeable changes are the omission of the screen device and the increase of scenes from seven to eight, but the publisher of the Acting Edition also notes that "the dialogue has to some extent been revised by the author." In the two principal studies to consider the changes in the texts, L. A. Beaurline finds that Williams shows his talent for brilliant dialogue in his final revisions, and Ruby Cohn notes that additions to Amanda's lines evoke pity and further endear her to us. The most significant thematic addition, however, has not been heretofore recognized. By numerous changes in dialogue Williams reveals his intention of developing the theme of the passing of good manners in modern America. Although he does not confine this quality to one part of the country, it is clear that he particularly associates it with the old South.

At the beginning of the first scene of the Library Edition the screen legend reads, "Où sont les neiges." In the Acting Edition at this point, Williams wrote a new opening speech of ten lines for

From *The Southern Literary Journal* 8, no. 2 (Spring 1976). ©1976 by *The Southern Literary Journal*.

Amanda in which her polite behavior contrasts with the rudeness she met at church. She tells Laura that the church was crowded except for one pew in which one little woman was sitting. She "smiled very sweetly" and said, "'Excuse me, would you mind if I shared this pew?'" The woman retorted that she certainly would since the space was rented. Amanda complains, "These Northern Episcopalians! I can understand the Southern Episcopalians, but these Northern ones, no." Since Williams stated that the screen device enabled him to rely less on "spoken lines," it is understandable that when he removed it here and elsewhere he often added dialogue.

In scene 3 of the Library Edition, when Amanda is promoting one of those serial sublimations of lady authors who think in terms of creamy thighs and caressing fingers, she calls it "the *Gone with the Wind* of the post-World War generation." In the Acting Edition, Williams replaces this comparison by Amanda's remark that it is all about "the horsey set on Long Island." As Williams makes Amanda more appealing and more complex by his final changes, he achieves the same end for the old South by omitting this unflattering reference to the most famous novel about that culture and by making subsequent additions.

The most important changes that Williams makes relate to Jim O'Connor. The alterations in his dialogue reduce his brashness and considerably increase his politeness, thus making him a model of good manners and a more sympathetic character. In the Library Edition when Amanda first meets Jim, the screen image shows "Amanda as a girl." This is replaced by Tom's flattering comment, "Mother, you look so pretty" and Amanda's reply, "You know, that's the first compliment you ever paid me." The stage is set for a flawless display of politeness by the characters who reenact the ways of the lady and her gentleman caller.

Jim's silences and raucous laughter in the Library Edition are replaced by courteous remarks and a decided increase in "ma'ams" in the Acting Edition. In the Library Edition, Jim says nothing while Amanda gives her lengthy welcome, but in the Acting Edition, he appropriately says, "How do you do?" In the next three pages of the Library Edition, Jim continues his silence; in the corresponding pages of the Acting Edition, he says "yes, ma'am" twice and "thank you, ma'am." Next in the opening pages of the last scene Jim's "ma'ams" are increased from three to eight and his two exclamations of "ha-ha" are replaced by courteous remarks, such as "Can I be of help, ma'am." In the Library Edition when Amanda tells her amusing story about the candelabrum of the Episcopal church getting melted, Jim responds, "Ha-ha," and nothing else is said in regard to this anecdote. In the Acting Edition, however, he asks, "Is that so, ma'am?" and Amanda says, "I never say anything that isn't so." He replies, "I beg your pardon." Then in the Library Edition, when Amanda asks if he can carry both the wine and candelabrum to Laura, he exclaims, "Sure. I'm Superman." This is changed to "I can try, ma'am." Through Jim, who is of Irish descent and lives in the North, Williams exemplifies politeness outside the South and prepares the way for predicting the fate of good manners in the whole country.

By a decisive addition, Williams pronounces an end to the good manners and hospitality associated with the old South. At the beginning of the last scene of the Library Edition the lights go out and the words "Suspension of a public service" appear on the screen. In the Acting Edition Williams adds five lines, starting with Amanda's comment that she has not had "such a pleasant evening in a very long time." Jim gallantly offers a toast "to the old South." Amanda responds, "The old South." Immediately there is a "blackout in both rooms." On leaving, Jim sums up what is passing with "a wonderful evening" such as this, "I guess this is what they mean by Southern hospitality."

The changes made in Jim's lines provide a sharper contrast to the future predicted for his personality. Like the hospitality of the old South, Jim's politeness seems destined for extinction. Although Laura tells him that she admired his "friendly way" in high school, he admits that he too had an inferiority complex then, and until he learned his aptitude for science never thought of himself as being "outstanding in any way whatsoever." Williams indicates that under the influence of someone like Amanda, who practices the good manners of former times, Jim's aptitude in that direction flourishes, but it is doomed by his ambitions for "*Money—Zzzzzzpp! POWER! Wham!*"

An awareness that Williams made important changes in the text of *The Glass Menagerie* is particularly needed because the Library Edition is much more often printed than the Acting Edition. The latter as a separate volume exists only in the text published for actors by

the Dramatists Play Service and is not as likely to be in college librar-
ies as is the New Directions reprint. A survey of anthologies reveals
that editors choose the Library Edition by a ratio of at least two to
one. Critics also are much more prone to use the Library Edition. If
readers use the Library Edition exclusively, they will remain igno-
rant of important additions to the dialogue decided on by Williams.

The Southern Gentlewoman

Signi Falk

Like D. H. Lawrence, Tennessee Williams, the son of a Puritanical mother and a boisterous father, was strongly attached to his mother during a serious childhood illness, later rebelled against her moral restrictions, and glorified the sensual. Williams's studies of Southern gentlewomen, his most distinctive contribution to the American theater, develop this conflict between the Puritan and the Cavalier that he had first portrayed in his earlier poems, short stories, and plays. Amanda Wingfield and her daughter Laura of *The Glass Menagerie,* Blanche DuBois of *A Streetcar Named Desire,* Alma Winemiller of *Summer and Smoke* and of *Eccentricities of a Nightingale,* and Hannah Jelkes of *The Night of the Iguana* are sympathetic variations of the type.

The conflict between the delicate person and the brutal one appears in the poem "Lament for Moths," a theme that dominates so much of Williams's work. Another poem, "Beanstalk Country," favorably contrasts the delicate and the slightly mad with the so-called normal. "Intimations" suggests a spinster poet far behind the times (*In the Winter of Cities*). The short story "A Portrait of a Girl in Glass" (*One Arm*), which is about the girl who retreats into her world of glass ornaments and phonograph records, is translated into Williams's first successful play. "The Resemblance between a Violin Case and a Coffin" (*Hard Candy*) describes the neurotic intensity and

From *Tennessee Williams* 2nd ed. ©1978 by G. K. Hall & Co.

the latent sensuousness of a girl emerging into her teens. "The Yellow Bird" (*One Arm*), a comic narrative that contrasts the Puritan-Cavalier tradition, ends in fantasy, as do *Summer and Smoke* and *Eccentricities of a Nightingale*. "The Case of the Crushed Petunias" (*American Blues*) is a comic portrayal of a shy miss who is rescued from the curse of virginity by a clumsy lover. The short story "The Night of the Iguana" (*One Arm*) tells of an oversexed Southern spinster who is released from her "rope of loneliness" by an attempted rape. In the one-act play *Portrait of a Madonna* (*27 Wagons Full of Cotton*), an aging church worker, wracked by her religious teaching and by her sexual dreams, is led away by officers of an asylum.

The Southern gentlewomen also represent the culture and the gentility, sometimes rather seedy, that disappeared during the decade of World War I. Though at times eccentric, these females are superior to the domesticated housewives and gossips who correspond to the average and the acceptable women. The male counterpart in this conflict is represented by young men who are sometimes attracted to this frustrated gentlewoman but who are sometimes almost emasculated by a domineering mother. The D. H. Lawrence derivative, the red-blooded symbol of sexual freedom who contrasts to the nondescript intellectual young man, sometimes establishes the conflict that is the essence of the play.

In the production notes to the first published edition of *The Glass Menagerie*, Williams expressed the hope that this "memory play" in seven sharply recreated scenes would anticipate "a new plastic theater" that would replace "the exhausted theater of realistic conventions." Since poetic imagination could transform the concrete into an inner truth, he rejected photographic realism in favor of unconventional techniques. In this same preface, his stage directions call for screen devices to project images and legends, for nostalgic music to enhance emotional overtones, and for shafts of light in different intensities to strengthen the dominant mood of a scene.

Tom Wingfield, an itinerant dreamer like his creator, is trapped not only in a monotonous warehouse job but also by responsibilities to his mother and his sister. Sometimes the narrator who introduces the scene and sometimes the actor in it, Tom sets the play in the 1930s. He describes Americans as going their blind way, dancing, making love, and as being mildly disturbed by labor troubles at the same time that the Spaniards are being methodically slaughtered at Guernica. A lonely soul, Tom is ignored or slightly ridiculed by his fellow workers at the plant where he works until the big Irishman, Jim O'Connor, pays attention to him.

Amanda Wingfield, the mother who is addicted to bromides and fantasies, is a middle-aged Southern belle. Garrulous and at times comic in her obsessions, her view of life is warped by her Puritan strictures; but she lives in delusions about her girlhood conquests. Her husband, present only in a blown-up photograph over the mantle, is described as a telephone man who fell in love with long distance and left his family for good. Deceived as a girl by his smile and uniform, she currently deludes herself about the seventeen gentleman callers who presented themselves one Sunday afternoon, men who later achieved wealth.

Just as willfully, Amanda ignores present reality. Overanxious to have her daughter, Laura, securely married, she refuses to recognize the girl's painful shyness or to admit to her slightly crippled leg. She insists that Laura not refer to herself as a cripple, that she speak only of a "little defect," and that she distract attraction from it by developing charm and vivacity. Amanda has known what can happen to a Southern girl without a home of her own: "I know so well what becomes of unmarried women who aren't prepared to occupy a position. I've seen such pitiful cases in the South—barely tolerated spinsters living upon the grudging patronage of sister's husband or brother's wife!—stuck away in some little mouse-trap of a room— encouraged by one in-law to visit another—little birdlike women without any nest—eating the crust of humility all their life!"

Though Amanda is proud of Tom, she is insensitive to his position. She carps at him continually about his eating habits, his smoking, his going to the movies, his late hours, his boredom with the warehouse job, and his need for adventure. When he tries to explain that man is by instinct a fighter, a hunter, and a lover, she is offended by his language. Reflecting her early twentieth-century Puritanism, Amanda believes that Christian adults should be concerned with things of the mind and spirit and leave dirty words like *instinct* for monkeys and pigs. Another argument erupts over a D. H. Lawrence novel that Tom brought home from the library, for she dismisses this writer as insane and offensive.

Exasperated by his mother's everlasting nagging about his running away to the movies, Tom bluntly tells her how much he detests the life he is leading. He is appalled by the idea of spending fifty-five years cooped up in a celotex workroom with fluorescent lights for sixty-five dollars a month; of waking up every morning to her maddening cheerfulness, "Rise and shine, rise and shine"; of returning each day to the warehouse, over and over again, in order to record shoe numbers. He would rather be dead. Tom Wingfield is a poet-dreamer who is something like his creator who also struggled against routine and conformity. Tom's shoe factory job, the poetry writing, the cramped living quarters, and the very close relationship with the sister are all echoes of Williams's own experience.

Laura, the morbidly shy and overly delicate sister, is as fragile as the little glass ornaments and phonograph records that are her escape. Through her timidity, her suffering from the friction between Tom and Amanda, and her retreat into a world of dreams, Laura evokes genuine sympathy; she is the one who must be cared for, loved, and understood. Her charm and delicacy win the audience, just as they have won her brother. Perceptive of others' feelings, Laura senses her mother's need to romanticize her past and so stands as a buffer between the mother and son. For one so sensitive and shy, the clanking brace on her leg is torture. During her final semester in high school, she becomes nervously ill, fails her final examinations, and does not graduate. When her desperate mother spends fifty dollars on a secretarial course, Laura becomes nauseated during the typing speed test. Amanda forces her to join a young people's church group where she might meet some nice boys. Because Laura won't or can't talk, the girl is humiliated.

The mother makes another attempt to provide for her daughter by asking Tom to find a clean-living, nondrinking suitor. When from his limited acquaintance he invites a warehouse friend to dinner, her hopes skyrocket. Tom admits that he has said nothing about Laura and tries to make his mother be a little more realistic:

> TOM: Mother you mustn't expect too much from Laura.
> AMANDA: What do you mean?
> TOM: Laura seems all those things to you and me because
>   she's ours and we love her. We don't even notice
>   she's crippled any more.
> AMANDA: Don't say crippled! You know that I never
>   allow that word to be used!

TOM: But face the facts, Mother. She is and—that's
  not all—
AMANDA: What do you mean, not all?
TOM: Laura is very different from other girls.
AMANDA: I think the difference is all to her advantage.
TOM: Not quite all—in the eyes of others—strangers—
  she's terribly shy and lives in a world of her own and
  those things make her seem a little peculiar to people
  outside the house.
AMANDA: Don't say peculiar.
TOM: Face the facts. She is.

Refusing to listen, Amanda tries with grim feminine energy to change Laura into a pretty trap; for, on the ill-fated evening when the girl is so nervously ill that she cannot eat dinner, the determined mother crudely isolates the young man and her daughter.

Tom describes Jim O'Connor, the gentleman caller, as a high-school hero; he was evidently one of those dynamic extroverts whose youth, looks, and enthusiasm won him the vote as the boy graduate most likely to succeed. Time and circumstances have proven otherwise, but he does work on self-improvement courses in public speaking and in radio engineering. Jim, the very average white-collar worker, the not too imaginative American, is, ironically, the boy whom Laura has secretly loved for years; but her only association with him has been his several pictures in the high-school annual.

Amanda's planned evening, begun in panic for Laura, becomes her dream made real for a brief time. It is a beautiful love scene set to candlelight—of necessity, since the electricity was turned off because Tom had appropriated the money to buy a merchant seaman's membership. When Laura brings out the high-school annual with all its romantic memories, she restores some of the old excitement to the disappointed hero. He brashly analyzes Laura as a victim of an inferiority complex, talks to her as if he were addressing his public-speaking class in evening school, and is completely impervious to the reactions of his little one-girl, wide-eyed audience. He says that she has magnified her trouble with the brace, that she ought to forget it, and that she should think of herself as superior in some way. Jim then talks in big terms about his own future plans, becomes a little abashed at his own egotism, and then remembers his evening class lesson about success that comes from interest in other people.

Laura responds to Jim's encouragement by showing him her precious glass collection. After she picks up her dearest treasure, the thirteen-year old unicorn, she points to the single horn on his forehead; she admits that he is extinct, but she asserts that she loves him because he must feel lonesome. This little glass figure is a living thing to her; she talks about his accepting without complaint his companions—horses without horns:

LAURA: Hold him over the light, he loves the light! You
see how the light shows through him?
JIM: It sure does shine!
LAURA: I shouldn't be partial, but he is my favorite one.
JIM: What kind of thing is this one supposed to be?
LAURA: Haven't you noticed the single horn on his
forehead?
JIM: A unicorn, huh?
LAURA: Mn—hmmmmmmmmm.
JIM: Unicorns, aren't they extinct in the modern world?
LAURA: I know!
JIM: Poor little fellow, he must feel sort of lonesome.
LAURA (smiling): Well, if he does he doesn't complain
about it. He stays on the shelf with some horses that
don't have horns and all of them seem to get along
nicely together.

Laura is carried away with the conversation, but Jim's attention is soon distracted by the music from across the alley. He gallantly asks Laura to dance; they take a few steps in a clumsy waltz and hit the table. There is a shatter of glass. The unicorn is broken.

LAURA: Now it is just like all the other horses.
JIM: It's lost its—
LAURA: Horn! It doesn't matter. Maybe it's a blessing in
disguise.
JIM: You'll never forgive me. I bet it was your favorite
piece of glass.
LAURA: I don't have favorites much. It's no tragedy,
Freckles. Glass breaks so easily. No matter how
careful you are.

Jim is won by Laura's unique charm, but he is even more impressed with his own power. Like the clumsy stumble-bum who broke the unicorn, and seemingly unaware of what has happened to the girl, he talks about making her proud and not shy. He kisses her and then realizes his mistake; for, seeing her bright, dazed look, he dimly senses her love for him. After he pops a mint into his mouth, he bluntly explains that another girl has strings on him. Unaware that he is destroying all the self-confidence that he might have built up in the girl, he talks of the power of love that has made a man of him. The playwright says of his heroine that the holy candles have been snuffed out, that her face has *"a look of almost infinite desolation."* Laura gently places the broken unicorn that has lost its unique quality and any resemblance to her in the hand of the big Irishman and closes his fingers around her favorite ornament. He seems unaware that he has broken not only her unicorn but also her heart.

When Amanda discovers the awful conclusion to her planned evening, she brutally accuses Tom of allowing them to make fools of themselves and of recklessly spending their slim resources; she has completely forgotten that Tom had tried to reason with her. When he leaves abruptly to escape to the movies, Amanda, left alone, comforts her wounded Laura; and her reassurances are strong enough to bring a smile to the girl's face. The tragic dignity of this brief scene, when Amanda's speech cannot be heard, recalls her earlier observation about Southern gentlewomen without a home of their own.

Tom, fired for writing poetry on the boss's time, leaves his home, as did his father, to find escape. He cannot succeed, for he finds in every city there is a reminder of his sister: "Oh, Laura, Laura, I tried to leave you behind me, but I am more faithful than I intended to be! I reach for a cigarette, I cross the street, I run into the movies or a bar, I buy a drink. I speak to the nearest stranger— anything that can blow your candles out! (LAURA *bends over the candles.*)—for now the world is lit by lightning! Blow out your candles, Laura—and so goodbye—(*She blows the candles out.*)"

The Glass Menagerie came into the American theater like a fresh spring wind. An original play that was about a part of the country not then well known, and that was cast and directed by the best talents, it became an exciting experience for many theatergoers. Despite Williams's distaste for the photographic, his play presents a good blend of imagination and realism; but it has overtones that are more complex than immediately apparent. One critic referred to the "unforgettable fragrance and glow" that Laurette Taylor gave to Amanda, "a poignantly pathetic figure" who evokes compassion, never scorn. Every actress who later played this complex role gave it a slightly different dimension, some emphasizing the humor, others the pathos.

Stark Young, who came from the same locality as Tennessee Williams, found all the language and motifs "free and true," and he believed the Southern speech of Amanda to be "the echo of great literature, or (to indicate) at least a respect for it." He said, "No role could be more realistically written," with variety and the "almost unconscious freedom, perhaps, of true realism." He felt, however, that since both son and father were born wanderers and adventurers, their parallels should have been heightened. Many comments about the original production suggest a too close attention to the theatrical effects called for by the playwright.

Later critics, who compared the original production with the revivals, agreed that time had not weakened the play "in spite of the sentimental patina." Writing about the twentieth-anniversary revival of this play, critics agreed that, although the play might be called a dream, it contained more information about its people than had Arthur Miller's Willy Loman in *Death of a Salesman*. One wrote that Williams's play "transforms autobiography into lucid, objective art," and that beneath the honest portrayal lies an awareness that there are "no solutions, nor exits from necessity." Another referred to the "play's lyricism . . . which ennobled the writer's bitter recollection of his youth." Another, commenting about the best of Williams in the "lightning flashes of things instantly recognized," calls attention to the scene when Tom, maddened by his mother's carping, screams at her about his wild life—all fiction.

Close to the third anniversary of the Chicago opening of *The Glass Menagerie* and shortly before the New York opening of *A Streetcar Named Desire,* Williams wrote an essay, "On a Streetcar Named Success," in which he commented on the shock of fame. The reception of the earlier play terminated one part of his life and began a very different one: from oblivion and from scratching for a living to "sudden prominence"; from a precarious tenancy in rented rooms to a suite in a first-class hotel with room service; from casual dress to expensive clothes. Success descended like a gloom; he was to recall "an ominous let down of spirit followed me like my shadow." He found that "success brings leeches" and makes a person a "public

Somebody," a fiction created by mirrors. His own "well of cynicism" frightened him; he suspected praise as flattery; he hated to respond to the repeated enthusiasm over *Menagerie*. After three months of this kind of "popularity," he retreated to the hospital for an eye operation; then he went to St. Louis, where he met William Inge, an aspiring playwright; and he sojourned in Chapala, Mexico, where he wrote *The Poker Night,* which was later incorporated into *A Streetcar Named Desire.* As he was to admit later, "once . . . (one) fully apprehend(s) the vacuity of a life without struggle," one recognizes that luxury, not poverty, is "the wolf at the door." He joined William James in calling success the "bitch goddess."

Celebration of a Certain Courage

C. W. E. Bigsby

[Tennessee Williams's] one-act play, "If You Breathe, it Breaks! or Portrait of a Girl in Glass," offers a more optimistic version of *The Glass Menagerie*. In that version Mrs Wingfield is the widow of an Episcopal clergyman, living in reduced circumstances and surviving by running a boarding house. She has two sons and a daughter, Rosemary, who is "a rather unearthly young person. She is overly delicate like a piece of glass too finely spun in very pale, transparent colors. Her survival in a world that has too little regard for delicate things will depend entirely upon the bare possibility of her discovering somebody who is willing to stand between her and the shattering impact of experience." Her brother is equally delicate and is rejected by the army. But in this play Rosemary finds the person she is looking for, while her brother finds contentment in his music. This was not a conclusion which he allowed to stand when he revised the play.

What he celebrates in *The Glass Menagerie* is a certain courage ("the most magnificent thing in all human nature is valor—and endurance," he once remarked) and, finally, a compassion that wins out over self-interest, despair and cruelty. Thus he tells us in a stage direction at the end of the play that "the interior scene is played as though viewed through soundproof glass. Amanda appears to be making a comforting speech to Laura who is huddled upon the sofa. Now that we cannot hear the mother's voice, her silliness is gone and

From *A Critical Introduction to Twentieth Century American Drama*. Vol. 2, *Tennessee Williams, Arthur Miller, Edward Albee*. ©1984 by C. W. E. Bigsby. Cambridge University Press, 1984.

she has dignity and tragic beauty. Laura's dark hair hides her face until at the end of the speech she lifts it to smile at her mother." *The Glass Menagerie* was an attempt to lay the ghosts of his own past. It was a play which he, like his protagonist, had to write and it was not for nothing that he gave his poet his own name. It was also a play which, in its elegiac tone, dramatised his problematic relationship to the past—personal and cultural. And the past has always been a major concern of the Southern writer.

The South that Williams pictures is either disintegrating, its moral foundations having been disturbed, or being taken over by the alienated products of modern capitalism. On the one hand are the rich, cancerous, their economic power signalled, in Lawrencian manner, through sexual impotence as in *Orpheus Descending,* or incestuous passion as in *Suddenly Last Summer* and *Sweet Bird of Youth*; on the other hand are the new, brutal proletariat, as in *A Streetcar Named Desire,* who begin by destroying a South become decadent and end, in *The Red Devil Battery Sign,* by destroying even themselves. It is a Spenglerian vision. Williams's sensibility was in an almost permanent state of recoil. The collapse of the South, though by no means unambiguous, is in some ways seen as the collapse of culture. The process is irresistible. What interests Williams is how the individual will negotiate a temporary reprieve from the progress of history and time. The uncoiling of the spring of history deconstructs the grace of youth, attenuates the urgent, authentic passions and subtle illusions with which the individual and state alike began. His characters exist in a world "sick with neon," in which pastel shades have for the most part deferred to primary colours, the wistful music of Laura's theme (in *The Glass Menagerie*) or the Vasouviana (in *Streetcar*) being superseded by the rhythms of the dance-hall band. And that music forges a link between Miller and Williams, who both locate their characters in the same no-man's-land, stranded between the real and the imagined, the spiritual and the material, a discordant present and a lyric nostalgia. Hence the flute music heard in *Death of a Salesman* is described by Miller as recalling "grass, and trees and the horizon," a lost world of lyricism and beauty confused with sadness, while the distant music of *The Glass Menagerie* is intended by Williams as "the lightest, most delicate music in the world and perhaps the saddest." It is "like circus music," heard "not when you are on the grounds or in the immediate vicinity of the parade, but when you are at some distance and very likely thinking of something else. . . . It expresses the surface vivacity of life with the underlying strain of innumerable and inexpressible sorrows." "Nostalgia," he suggests, "is the first condition of the play," as it is in a sense of all Williams's work, but it is a nostalgia for a past which he could not entirely convince himself had ever existed. Like Miller's Willy Loman, his characters find themselves hopelessly stranded in a kind of temporal and spatial void. They can relate neither to their setting nor to the times in which they find themselves living, and thus they fill that void with distorted memories of the past, or wistful dreams of a redemptive future. But they have no more connection with past or future than they do with the present. In both *The Glass Menagerie* and *Death of a Salesman* time boundaries have dissolved. The tension which holds past and present apart has gone. The imagination is the only resource, but the imagination is equally a product of paranoia; it is in some degree primary evidence of the collapse of structure. It becomes a kind of hysterical or neurotic spasm which can no longer be controlled because there is no longer an available model of order, of social or moral imperatives, which can command respect and authority.

There is a brief essay by Tennessee Williams which does much to explain not only his sense of theatre but also his perception of the ironies of life. As with O'Neill, these ironies can generate either tragic insight or an absurdist despair, but at their heart is an implacable fear of time. For

> it is this continual rush of time, so violent that it appears to be screaming, that deprives our actual lives of so much dignity and meaning, and it is, perhaps more than anything else, the *arrest of time* which has taken place in a completed work of art that gives to certain plays their feeling of depth and significance.
>
> (*Five Plays by Tennessee Williams*)

Time is, indeed, the dominant fact in all of his work. The pressure of time prompts the lies and evasions which themselves become the basis for misunderstandings and despair. The undeniable reality of time drains individual actions of significance. By the same token the suspension of time in a play, or perhaps its radical foreshortening, permits the writer and his audience to abstract the individual from the obscuring random occurrences of everyday life in order to detect meaning in the heart of chaos and to give value to those lives behind by the rush of history. For Williams, if only Miller's Willy Loman could have been encountered "outside of time," he could have prompted the concern, the kindness and even respect which was his due as an individual. Inside of time he becomes an irrelevance, a trivial cog in a machine whose relentless rhythm is alien to his own needs. The mere act of relocating him in artistic time thus becomes an assertion of values. The writer gives dignity to his characters by writing about them; he emphasizes the insidious but invisible effect of time by suspending it.

This concern with time is deeply rooted in a personal neurosis about mortality which took Williams to the psychiatrist's couch and to the physician's office. But it is hardly irrelevant to his sense of a culture in which impermanence had been established as an economic and aesthetic value, and which for many people set the pace for modernity. And while admitting that passion is no less ephemeral than the facts it wishes to deny, he insists that that ephemerality "should not be regarded as proof of its inconsequence." For the "great and only possible dignity of man lies in his power deliberately to choose certain moral values by which to live as steadfastly as if he, too, like a character in a play, were immured against the corrupting rush of time." So, while, "as far as there exists any kind of empiric evidence, there is no way to beat the game of *being* against *non-being*, in which non-being is the pre-destined victor on realistic levels," it is still possible to snatch "the eternal out of the desperately fleeting." This is "the great magic trick of human existence." And so the "trick" of the artist becomes paradigmatic; the act of invention becomes crucial to survival and personal meaning, and the imagination a vital instrument of redemption. And yet, by freezing time, art mimics the death which it is designed to deny—that is the paradox at the heart of his work. For, if the imagination can generate a momentary meaning, it can also compound the forces it would neutralize. As Williams remarks, "Fear and evasion are the two little beasts that chase each other's tails in the revolving wire-cage of our nervous world. They distract us from feeling too much about things. Time rushes towards us with its hospital tray of infinitely varied narcotics, even while it is preparing us for its inevitably fatal operation" (*Where I Live*). This is the temptation to which Laura succumbs in *The Glass Menagerie,* but the alternative is equally chilling and she is unwilling to surrender her dreams for the prosaic world of the typing pool and the frightening causalities of time.

Laura's unicorn can only survive by relinquishing its horn, thereby joining the homogenised world of the horses, but Williams's characters are not free to make the choice. The imaginative perception and sexual potency which make them so vulnerable stand as images of the creative sensibility. And to that extent all Williams's plays are in effect about the plight of the writer—a special individual whose vocation demands a willed openness of spirit that makes him a natural victim of the pressure of events. It is, perhaps, for that reason that in *The Glass Menagerie* he deliberately foregrounds technique, makes his methods apparent and therefore, in a sense, his subject. Nor was Williams unaware of the irony that the act of writing, which, in the preface to *The Glass Menagerie,* he saw as an attempt to catch the organic nature of "truth, life, or reality" by an act of imaginative transformation, is also unavoidably an escape from those objectives, a denial of their force as totally determining realities. Tom's opening speech in *The Glass Menagerie* contains an implicit attack on America. The collapse of the old world left only a sense of baffled incomprehension, while in Spain a battle was on to construct a new future. But, for all his rhetoric, it was not a battle that Tom was constitutionally fitted to join. And much the same could be said of Williams himself, whose story, in effect, this was. For he, too, after his early, directly social plays was, in effect, retreating from the battle, turning to words. By degrees he negotiated a retreat from the immediate issues of social injustice, from the need to use art as an instrument of social and moral analysis, and instead used it increasingly as a mirror in which he saw his own sense of desperation and alienation. His became a dark world which could no longer be lit up by the clear light of political commitment or an assertive moral passion, but only by the brief sparks of imagination or the reflective glow of a past which he chose to invest with an energy and radiant truth in which, in other moods, he could not bring himself to believe.

The Glass Menagerie is not narrated by a confident voice. Tom is as lost in the supposed present as he had been in the recalled past. Imagining that the suffocation of his spirit, the warping of his ideals, and the stultification of his aspirations were a product of his physical environment, he had broken free. But his freedom, like that invoked by Miller's Linda at the end of *Death of a Salesman,* is an ironic one. The space which he needed was not a physical one after all. Like Albee's Jerry, in *The Zoo Story,* he comes to realize that all his retreat from human relationships has won him is "solitary free passage." If, in the words of one of Sartre's characters, "hell is other people," he has found that hell is also isolation, so that now he is forced to people his world with memories and to acknowledge that he has stumbled on a further paradox: for his escape ties him to the past even more firmly. It creates a sense of guilt, which makes it impossible ever to evade the demands that in some way are the price of one's humanity. And so not only is Tom forced to relive the past from which he thought he had escaped, but, in *A Streetcar Named Desire,* Blanche DuBois is equally haunted by her own failure to acknowledge a human responsibility—a failure which sends her, too, on a desperate and hopeless flight.

The gentleman caller, invoked by Amanda to give dignity to her past and substance to Laura's future, is both "an emissary from a world of reality" and "a symbol" of "the long delayed but always expected something that we live for." And as such he is indicative of the limits of the imagination. The Wingfields cannot finally make him into something which he is not, although he, too, in the form of the young Jim O'Connor, brought home by Tom as a potential husband for his sister, is trapped in the process of constructing another series of dreams, believing that mastery of public speaking will place the world at his command. He wishes to identify with what Spengler had called the "Age of the Caesars." For him, as for Spengler, the new spirit of the age is dominated by *"Knowledge! . . . Money! . . . Power!"* And as such, even unknowingly, he destroys the subtle and the gentle and the maimed. But he, too, is a victim of his own dreams, slipping ever further behind in what he believes to be a crucial race for success.

Laura is a loving portrait of Williams's own sister locked up in her own inner world, her lobotomy trapping her in a permanent adolescence. It is a withdrawal from sociality for which Williams offers a gentler image, in terms of Laura's limp, an imperfection less intrusive, less totally disabling, but the play is a homage to her. Indeed, in a sense the various puns on her real name, Rose, are a writer's private acknowledgment of guilt and love. But all of Williams's characters are crippled in one sense or another—emotionally, spiritually—and out of that imperfection there comes a need which generates the illusions with which they fill their world, the art which they set up against reality. Like Laura's glass animals, however, those illusions and that art prove fragile.

For Williams, narrative itself is the origin of painful ironies. It implies causality, the unravelling of a time which can only be destructive of character and relationship. It is, in a sense, the guarantee of a final victory for death. Hence he and his characters try to stop time. They react, in a sense, against plot. In a way the narrative of their lives does not generate meaning; the meaning ascribed to those lives by history and myth generates the narrative. And as a result they wish to freeze the past and inhabit it, or they spin their own autonomous fictions and submit themselves to a logic dictated by symbol and metaphor. The virtue of the glass menagerie, for Laura, is precisely that it is inanimate. So, too, Blanche's Belle Reve, by turns the family plantation and her own system of illusions, is indestructible and unchanging so long as it can be preserved from assault by the real. Yet if that symbol is put under too great a stress then the only remaining recourse lies in flight, a fluidity of identity and event which appears to offer some kind of defence. And his characters do tend to opt for a world in which their personal outline becomes blurred. They lose definition, indeed they fear definition. Laura, her mother asserts, is "not a cripple." Blanche is not a sexual tramp. But if these evasions are necessary they are also destructive, for, without definition, they are without self. At the end of *The Glass Menagerie* the candles of Laura's life are snuffed out. At the end of *Streetcar* Blanche is taken off to an equally lobotomized existence. They now inhabit their fictions entirely. They are invulnerable to further assault, but their invulnerability is the mark of their destruction, of the loss of their humanity. For that is one more paradox which Williams explores in his work. To exist is to be vulnerable. In the words of one of Albee's characters, existence is pain. Narcosis is no solution in that it resolves the paradox by destroying one of its components. The problem is to find a response that permits of both form and movement. And this is equally the problem for the playwright. The solution to which both Miller and Williams were drawn was the "memory play," in which the hard edge of reality could be balanced by an imaginative freedom. Constraining walls suddenly become translucent. Time, for a moment, becomes plastic, malleable; indeed it is set into reverse. In *Death of a Salesman* the surrounding apartments disappear amidst a kaleidoscope of leaves; in *A Streetcar Named Desire* the domestic squalor of the apartment is bathed suddenly in a glow produced by Blanche's silk scarf draped over a lamp, an effect which reminds her of the soft lights that illuminated her youth. In

The Glass Menagerie candlelight abstracts the characters for a moment from an all too literal present. As Jo Mielziner, designer of the stage sets for many of Williams's plays, has remarked,

> If he had written plays in the days before the technical development of translucent and transparent scenery, I believe he would have invented it. . . . My use of translucent and transparent scenic interior walls was not just another trick. It was a true reflection of the contemporary playwright's interest in—and at times obsession with—the exploration of the inner man. Williams was writing not only a memory play but a play of influences that were not confined within the walls of a room.
>
> *(Designing for the Theatre)*

Writing to Donald Windham in 1943, Williams had complained that *The Gentleman Caller* lacked the violence that usually excited him, but in the final version his achievement lay in the drama which he created out of stasis.

The Glass Menagerie was a considerable success. It ran for 561 performances, finally closing in August 1946 after a run of some sixteen months. It won the New York Critics' Circle Award as well as the *Catholic Monthly* and Sidney Howard Memorial awards. George Jean Nathan attributed some of its success to the play's director, Dowling, who had resisted Williams's desire to have captions projected onto a screen at the rear of the stage, and who, he suggested, had invented the scene in which Laura sits on the fire escape and listens to the music from the dance hall, a scene which he found one of "the most touching" in the play. But he admired Williams's work while resisting what he felt was a lack of generosity towards his collaborators. Williams's version was wholly different. He insisted that the scene in question was actually the invention of Nathan and Dowling together who concocted it over drinks in a hotel room. Not yet in a position to resist such pressures Williams himself rewrote the scene, and it was retained in the script where the most he could bring himself to say of it was that it did the play little harm. His own doubts centered around the narrations which he continued to believe detracted from the play's power.

To a degree Williams's turn from a public to a private world was itself a response to profound changes in society itself. The American poster designer E. McKnight Kauffer, in an address which he gave to the Royal Society of Arts as early as 1938, observed that,

> with the world as it is, and social values what they are, there is an almost inevitable tendency for a private world. I cannot help feeling myself that external reality has to some extent lost something of its collective significance, or perhaps it is that its significance seems less valuable and less immediate in its appeal, contrasted with the distress that social disruption on such a colossal scale as we have witnessed in our time, has created.

And in a sense *The Glass Menagerie* and the plays which followed can be seen as a displaced response to social forces which he had earlier chosen to engage on the level of politics. In 1945, he observed:

> Today we are living in a world which is threatened by totalitarianism. The Fascist and the Communist states have thrown us into a panic of reaction. Reactionary opinion descends like a ton of bricks on the head of any artist who speaks out against the current of prescribed ideas. We are all under wraps of one kind or another, trembling before the specter of investigating committees and even with Buchenwald in the back of our minds.
>
> *(Where I Live)*

His response to this, however, was no longer to confront that coercion directly or to examine it for its economic content but, "not to conform . . . the biologist will tell you that progress is the result of mutations . . . freaks." And so he celebrates that marginal figure, the character who finds himself, or more frequently herself, at odds with a world which is seen as a threat. The tone of his essay seemed confident. In fact it was tinged with hysteria ("For God's sake let us defend ourselves against whatever is hostile to us without imitating the thing which we are afraid of!") and his characters seldom if ever prove equal to the task of resisting a coercive world. Certainly Laura is broken like her unicorn.

Writing of the American author Paul Bowles in 1950, Williams noted that he had substituted a concern with "the fearful isolation of the individual being" for that obsession with "group membership and purposes" which had typified writers in the 1930s. A similar substitution had characterized Williams's own work. Where in the early plays he celebrated a group of people who suffered through material deprivation, now he chose to write about the solitary individual or sometimes a sad alliance of two such people. And interestingly enough he argued that this shift was necessitated by the oppressive nature of American political life: "What choice has the artist, now, but withdrawal into the caverns of his isolated being?" It was the forces of reaction, he argued, which had created the vogue for what was assailed as decadence but which he preferred to characterize as lyricism. He, like Bowles, responded to what he called "the extreme spiritual dislocation . . . of our immediate times," which he saw as the product of "the social experience of two decades." But, in contrast to Bowles, he suggested that life nonetheless "achieves its highest value and significance in those rare moments— they are scarcely longer than that—when two lives are confluent, when the walls of isolation momentarily collapse between two persons." Laura knows such a moment, but it dissolves in her hands and sends her plunging back into an isolation which is all the deeper for her having glimpsed another possibility. This was to be a recurring irony in Williams's work as his imagination did battle with an increasing apocalypticism.

He was also inclined to see his own thematic concern with survival as a reflection of the political world which he had once addressed directly. For apocalypse was in the air. When he was writing *The Glass Menagerie* it was inherent in a war in which the fragile and the vulnerable were menaced by power. By 1950 he saw a more precise focus for this fear. As he wrote, "Everywhere the people seem to be waiting for the new cataclysm to strike them . . . they are waiting for it to happen with a feeling of fatality. . . . Nevertheless, the people want to survive, they want to keep on living through it, whatever it may be." And this, of course, was the primary objective of his own threatened characters. Yet what they fear is not simply or even primarily something in the social or political world for, as he insisted, "the true sense of dread is not a reaction to anything sensible or visible or even, strictly, materially, *knowable*. But rather it's a kind of spiritual intuition of something almost too incredible and shocking to talk about, which underlies the whole so-called thing." The only name he was prepared to give to this was "*mystery*" but in fact, as his work makes clear, it is time, mortality, and a failure of love to neutralise either of these forces.

Yet as late as 1952 he was still laying claim to a social consciousness which he regarded as the distinguishing characteristic of his work. Recalling the contrast between his family's relative poverty and the affluence which surrounded them, he insisted that it "produced a shock and a rebellion that has grown into an inherent part of my work. It was the beginning of the social consciousness which I think has marked most of my writing." Moreover, he insisted, "I am glad that I received this bitter education for I don't think any writer has much purpose back of him unless he feels bitterly the inequities of the society he lives in." And that pressure does survive in his work but, as in *The Glass Menagerie,* transmuted into a drama in which the fragile and the vulnerable are seen to be as much victims of their own dreams as of the implacable force of the real and the unforgiving rhythms of modernity. Laura cannot adjust to a world in which she must function as a typist or trade her delicate sensibility for security. The axes of her life are different from those which locate other people, so she steps out of time into a security as intransitive as it is total.

The Two Glass Menageries: Reading Edition and Acting Edition

Geoffrey Borny

I. FROM PAGE

The Glass Menagerie was rescued from possible oblivion in December 1944 by the almost unprecedented efforts of the Chicago critics who cajoled audiences to go and see the play. Since its rather faltering first appearance, the play has gone on to become a classic of American theatre. Like all classics it has had built up around it a body of criticism which has done as much to obscure the meaning of the play as to elucidate it. King rightly claims that "*The Glass Menagerie*, though it has achieved a firmly established position in the canon of American plays, is often distorted, if not misunderstood, by readers, directors and audiences."

One of the most enduring, and least endearing, critical standpoints that has guided generations of readers into seeing the play from a point of view different from that intended and created by the playwright has been the almost constant, and often unquestioned, assumption that Williams's strength lies in his ability to depict *realistic* characters and situations. Not surprisingly this same standpoint leads to a devaluation of all the "plastic" or "expressionistic" elements of his playwriting.

The major results of such a view of Williams would not have been quite so harmful had they stayed within the covers of books and

From *Page to Stage: Theatre as Translation*, edited by Ortrun Zuber-Skerritt. ©1984 by Editions Rodopi B. V.

articles about Williams. Unfortunately many directors seem to be influenced by the pro-realism critics, and often downplay or cut many of the more overtly expressionistic staging devices suggested by Williams as important for the play's production. Understandably audiences can appreciate only what is presented to them, and what is most often presented by directors of *The Glass Menagerie* is a kind of sentimental soap opera. An anonymous reviewer of the Broadway revival of the play succinctly sums up the result of ignoring the plastic/expressionistic elements of the play when he claims of Williams that

> his plays are seldom performed with the force, subtlety and imaginative risk-taking they require. Instead they have [been] . . . pushed toward realism, their complex truths dealt with as so much emotional merchandise to be peddled.

I am convinced that any downplaying in production of the expressionist elements in Williams's *Glass Menagerie* results in a trivialization of the play. I wished to see whether or not my thesis could be sustained and the acid test had to be a production of the play. Some of the hoary old critical clichés about the so-called weaknesses of Williams's expressionistic staging devices immediately come under close scrutiny the moment one examines the play in the theatre rather than simply in the study. Long revered critical judgements concerning *The Glass Menagerie* which appear on the face of it to be incontestable, turn out to be either of dubious validity or downright unworkable, when tested in the laboratory of the theatre.

Leacroft came to a similar conclusion concerning the famous drawings for the Tragic, Comic and Satyric scenes that appeared in Serlio's *Achitettura* (1545). When Leacroft tried to move from page to stage he found that the drawings were inconsistent with each other, a thing that no one had noticed before because no one had previously tested them.

> As is so often the case the preparation of a reconstruction—whether in the form of a drawing or a model—draws attention to discrepancies between drawings *which have been reproduced many times by historians without comment.*

Leacroft's comment certainly applies mutatis mutandis to the judgements of critics concerning Williams's use of nonrealistic staging techniques. Gassner's (*Masters of the Drama*) early attitude that "*The Glass Menagerie* was marred only by some preciosity, mainly in the form of stage directions, most of which were eliminated in Eddie Dowling's memorable Broadway production" is echoed, and echoed uncritically, by as important a critic as Styan in his recent three volume work on modern drama:

> From the German director Erwin Piscator he had borrowed the idea of scattering through the play titles and images projected on a screen, and Williams certainly thought of his episodic method as expressionistic. "Expressionism and all other unconventional techniques in drama have only one valid aim, and that is a closer approach to truth." Such devices were not an attempt to escape from reality, but to find "a more penetrating and vivid expression of things as they are." He also believed that they were a step towards "a new, plastic theatre," one replacing "the exhausted theatre of realistic conventions." This was the familiar tune, but in the event, the screen device got in the way of the direct impact of the play's action, and was wisely abandoned.

Styan's dismissive attitude towards those plastic expressionistic elements of Williams's dramaturgy is based on his theoretical predilection for dramas employing realistic techniques of both staging and dramaturgy. Styan thereby "saves" Williams from himself by transforming the American dramatist into a copy of Anton Chekhov:

> The non-realistic framework of the play, in which the son of the family, Tom Wingfield, plays chorus to the scenes of his memory, and even the Piscator devices of expressionistically projected titles and images (dropped in the New York production without damaging the fabric of the play), scarcely disturbed the Chekhovian detail of the main action.

Weales has taken into account the importance of both the realistic and nonrealistic elements of Williams's work:

> [Williams] has never been a realistic playwright . . . but he has always been capable of writing a psychologically valid scene in the American realistic tradition—the breakfast

scene in *The Glass Menagerie* for instance. . . . However grounded in realistic surface, the events in Williams' plays . . . take on meaning that transcends psychological realism.

Ten years earlier however, even Weales had implied that Williams's use of nonrealistic techniques was the weaker part of his work and specifically pointed out that it was realism that was central to the American theatrical tradition:

> In the Production Notes to *The Glass Menagerie* he [Williams] makes quite clear that he believes that poetic truth can best be depicted through a transformation that escapes the appearance of reality. Despite his aesthetic stand, he is enough in the tradition of the American theater to ask his characters to move and speak realistically when he wants them to.

Weales's slighting reference to Williams's "aesthetic stand" and Styan's even more dismissive reference to "the familiar tune" echo Gassner's charge of "preciosity." Each of these important critics recognizes that Williams has claimed that he is not a realist, yet all of them undervalue precisely those nonrealistic elements in Williams's work that lie outside the mainstream of the American theatre tradition. Williams is praised whenever his work fits the realistic tradition that Corrigan has called "the theater of verisimilitude [where] the settings, props, and lighting provide an environment for the action." Even as perceptive a critic as Eric Bentley asserts that "Williams can write very well when he writes realistically, when, for example, he writes dialogue based on observation of character; in fact, all his dramatic talent lies in that direction."

In my production of *The Glass Menagerie* I did not wish to challenge the obviously correct view that Williams did in fact write fine realistic dialogue and create convincing characters. Rather I wished to see whether or not the nonrealistic plastic/expressionistic elements so often dismissed by the major critics did have theatrical validity. In effect I wished to test who was the better judge of the play, the critics or the playwright himself.

When embarking on the production I accepted a directorial standpoint that assumed that there is such an entity as *the playwright's play*. With this in mind I tried to follow Williams's stated instructions as closely as possible. I fully accepted the relationship between director and playwright that is so lucidly expressed by Corrigan:

> In the theatre, the playwright must be the primary creator. His intention *must* be expressed in every aspect of production. . . . The chief aim of all the artists of the theatre must always be to realise that attitude toward life expressed by the playwright in his play.

I believe that it is only when a director utilises Williams's specified nonrealistic staging techniques in combination with actors creating their characters through the use of a realistic acting style that the audience can actually experience the play that Williams wrote.

The first thing that faces a director of *The Glass Menagerie* is that there are *two* published versions to choose between. The script that Eddie Dowling used in Chicago and later New York is not the version that is published in Williams's collected works. It is not true as Styan claims that Williams "wisely abandoned" the screen device and the other nonrealistic elements. The truth is that Williams wrote a more "acceptable," because more realistic, version of his play in order to get it performed. He in effect wrote an adaptation of *The Glass Menagerie* for the original performance *but* he chose to have his original play published in his collected works.

The version used by Eddie Dowling in the original production is the so-called Acting Edition published and commented on by the Dramatists Play Service Inc. This version

> differs from the book of the play as first issued by Random House: the dialogue itself has to some extent been revised by the author, and the stage directions likewise. The latter have been drastically changed in order to guide the director and actor.

The Acting Edition certainly is different from the Reading Edition. The director and actors are given a play that is much more realistic than the one published as the Reading Edition and republished in Williams's collected plays. To begin with in the Acting Edition, unlike the Reading Edition, there is no summary description of the characters preceding the play; the expressionistic stage devices are dispensed with; the expressionistic lighting plot is made more real-

istic; the transition between scenes is made less obviously artificial.
When one adds to this the fact that, as Beaurline noted, there are
"1100 verbal changes" that transform the characters, we can see that
we are dealing with two markedly different plays.

I chose to direct the Reading Edition both because Williams
seems to prefer this version and also because I think it is a much finer
play than the Acting Edition. The critics who prefer the Acting Edition usually do so because that version is more realistic. Rowland,
who made a study of the two versions of *The Glass Menagerie* using
the character of Amanda as the focus of his examination, claims that
the Amanda of the Acting Edition is

> more gentle, more loving and understanding . . . more
> conversational, more human, more realistic. . . . We see a
> more humble and practical Amanda in a more depressing
> and realistic world. . . . [She speaks] lines that are full of
> life and realism.

Ultimately Rowland rests his case concerning the "superiority" of
the Acting Edition over the Reading Edition on the grounds that the
Acting Version is more lifelike:

> The "reading version" gives Laura and Tom a stage com-
> panion. The "acting version" gives them a mother.

I don't contest that the Acting Edition may be more lifelike—more
realistic or that that version was well received by audiences. What I
do contest is the assumption that dramatic art is better the closer it
gets to verisimilitude. More precisely it seems to me that the harder
one pushes Williams's play towards realism the more one confuses
art with life and falsifies the vision of reality that he wished to drama-
tize. In his production notes to the play Williams explicitly defends
expressionism and attacks realism, as a means of expressing reality.
Williams, while vindicating the artist and denigrating the photogra-
pher, argues strongly that

> reality is an organic thing which the poetic imagination
> can represent, in essence only through transformation,
> through changing into other forms than those which were
> merely present in appearance.

Williams does not see his function as an artist simply in terms of
putting life on stage. He follows Aristotle's view that "poetry [art] is

something more philosophical and more worthy of serious attention than history; for while poetry is concerned with universal truths, history treats of particular facts." Williams does everything in his power to transcend the particular by using all the nonrealistic techniques he can to break the illusion of reality which is so beloved in the tradition of American realism. The mere accurate description of "a mother" is trivial for Williams who has always claimed that his concern as a dramatist was to master the "necessary trick of rising above the singular to the plural concern, from personal to general import."

Because Williams is so adept at writing realistic dialogue and creating convincingly real characters there is a great danger that the director and actors will emphasize these realistic elements at the cost of the nonrealistic ones. We need constantly in a production of *The Glass Menagerie* to remind ourselves that it is a work of art and not a slice of life. A play is, as Hethmon succinctly puts it, "in its very nature a symbolic representation of an individual action in relation to a system."

There seems to be little problem for critics and directors when dealing with either overtly realistic or overtly symbolic dramas. It is only in plays like *The Glass Menagerie* where realism and nonrealism are mixed, where, as Wimsatt puts it, "the order of images . . . follows or apparently follows the lines of representational necessity or probability, though at the same time a symbolic significance is managed" that problems of interpretation seem to occur.

It should be clear why I chose the Reading Edition in preference to the Acting Edition as the version I wished to direct. The Reading Version has within it a realistic story that is like life and has individual significance but because it is seen through a filter of nonrealistic staging devices and metafictional elements which draw attention to the fact that the play is a play, not a slice of life, the realistic story is made symbolically significant. It moves from the particular to the universal, from history to philosophy, from a representation of men to a representation of an action.

In directing *The Glass Menagerie* Reading Edition I did not undervalue the realistic characterization because any attempt to make symbolic puppets of characters like Amanda, Tom or Laura would be to make a travesty of the play. However, by equally emphasizing the nonrealistic and metafictional elements, I hoped to avoid the trap noted by Juneja when he accurately pointed out that "in *The Glass*

Menagerie it is the warm flesh and blood humanity of three dimensional characters that tends to mask the philosophic import of the play."

II. To Stage

Tom, the narrator, immediately sets up the metafictional nature of the play. Williams gives the actor playing Tom the stage direction: "He addresses the audience." This immediately breaks the fourth wall convention so central to realism. The fact that this is a "memory play" also means that historification takes place inducing a kind of alienation effect which controls the possible empathetic response that would otherwise occur. Empathy is inappropriate because it leads to an identification between the audience and the hero or heroine. What Williams requires is a degree of "distance" to allow the audience to see beyond the particular problems of his characters in order to perceive the symbolic truth of the action of the play. It is for this reason that Williams makes Tom both a character in the play and the narrator of the play. In his stage instructions Williams points out that "the narrator is an undisguised convention of the play. He takes whatever licence with dramatic convention is convenient to his purposes." In my production presented in a small proscenium arch theatre, I emphasized this conventional use of the narrator figure by having Tom enter through the audience, click his fingers as a signal for the curtain to rise, and then climb up the fire-escape steps onto the stage itself. The aim of this entrance was to immediately establish for the audience that the theatre, including the auditorium in which they were sitting, was a world that they shared with the narrator. The characters in the play, who are figments of the narrator's memory, all existed only on the stage and so they never entered the auditorium or played directly to the audience. The characters in Tom's "memory play" become distanced and objectified no matter how realistically they are played by the actors because they are seen through the mediating sensibility of the often ironically humorous narrator.

Having Tom click his fingers and "magically" having the curtain rise helped to overcome the first problem of the play. Tom's opening line is difficult for an actor to justify as it appears to be an answer to an implied question from the audience:

TOM: Yes, I have tricks in my pocket, I have things up my
  sleeve.

The "trick" of raising the curtain and then the immediate turning to
the audience to explain this behaviour overcomes this problem. Immediately the rules of the theatre game that is being played are established. Williams has Tom point out that although he does have all the
"tricks" of the theatrical trade he is "the opposite of the stage magician." He gives you illusion that has the appearance of truth. "I give
you truth in the pleasant disguise of illusion." Realism, which attempts to create an illusion of reality, has only the surface appearance
of truth, but through employing nonrealistic theatrical fictions Williams, through his alter-ego Tom, will depict the truth. This opening
speech is a direct attack on the inadequacies of realism and therefore
anything that can be legitimately used in actual production to stop
audiences reading the play as a slice of life is justifiable. Tom's preference for nonrealism as a mode for embodying truth echoes what
Schlueter has called "the phenomenon of self-consciousness which
characterizes so much of modern art." She outlines what Williams as
an artist dramatizes, namely the bankruptcy of realism as a mode for
expressing anything truthful about life:

> While the great tradition of Western literature willingly ac-
> cepts fiction as reality, the "other tradition" bases itself on
> the logical possibility that, since fictions are not real—a
> work of art comes closer to the truth of reality when it
> does not pretend to be what it is not, but rather declares
> itself to be what it is.

So Tom begins *The Glass Menagerie* by saying what the play *is*, not
life but art. In life time goes relentlessly forward. The world of the
play is not bound by such limitations. As Tom points out: "To begin
with I can turn back time." What is important to note here is that, in
production, the audience is aware of two time scales—the present in
which they and the narrator exist and the past in which the other
characters exist. Spectators are also made aware that they are present
in two places: in a theatre in Armidale and in a slum apartment in St
Louis. In life one cannot be in two places at once nor in one place at
two times. In art which does not try to be life but draws attention to
its own artifice, both things are possible.

In life events are not normally accompanied by music but in Williams's play music not only occurs but, as if to emphasize the artifice of such a convention, Tom is made to draw attention to its use:

> (*Music begins to play*). The play is memory. Being a memory play, it is dimly lighted, it is sentimental, it is not realistic. In memory everything happens to music. That explains the fiddle in the wings.

We all of us have seen films where the music which we are largely unaware of carries us along on a tide of emotion. We might also remember the effect in Mel Brooks's *Blazing Saddles* where the music's typical emotional evocation of the wide open prairies is undercut when the camera forces us to see the whole of the Count Basie band playing in the middle of the Wild West! Williams's use of music is closer to the Mel Brooks variety. I chose extremely sentimental romantic music for Amanda in several phrases taken from Paganini's Violin Concertos. The idea was to back up Amanda's reveries but at the same time to allow Tom and the nonrealistic stage devices to function as Williams intended them to do by ironically undercutting the scenes in which Amanda waxes lyrical.

In scene 1 we have a perfect example of Williams's ability to give his audience a twofold perspective. He allows the actress playing Amanda to play the character's own reality with honest sentiment while at the same time having Tom as the narrator, and the stage devices reduce this sentiment to sentimentality.

> (*She addresses* TOM *as though he were seated in the vacant chair at the table though he remains at the portieres. He plays this scene as though reading from a script.*)
> My callers were gentleman callers—all! Among my callers were some of the most prominent young planters of the Mississippi Delta—planters and sons of planters! (TOM *motions for music and a spot of light on* AMANDA. *Her eyes lift, her face glows, her voice becomes rich and elegiac.*)
> (SCREEN LEGEND: OÙ SONT LES NEIGES D'ANTAN?) There was young Champ Loughlin.

The first important thing that I noticed in production was that the metafictional elements and expressionistic stage devices paradoxically allowed the actors to play their own roles totally realistically.

They had no need to supply any ironic comments on their own behaviour as these were supplied by the narrator and his bag of theatrical tricks. When the play is presented without the ironical undercutting, it either becomes unbearably sentimental or the actors themselves have to include in their own performances some ironical undercutting.

In the scene just quoted I had Tom as the narrator resignedly mouthing a couple of Amanda's lines as she spoke them to indicate that he had heard this "script" so many times that he knew it by heart. The spotlight and romantic music should not come in unnoticed. I had Tom click his fingers again to "magically" produce these theatrical effects. All the while the actress playing Amanda was asked to play the truth of her character. She certainly does not see herself as ridiculous. The screen image is the final, and to my mind perfect, means of deflating Amanda's pretentions. We take the same ironical view of Amanda as Tom does in his memory. These much maligned screen legends are not, as some critics seem to suppose, ponderously serious captions supplying some sort of Brechtian "gestus" for each scene. In this scene the screen legend has a humorous deflating function allowing an audience to see the pathetically romantic pretentiousness of Amanda as Tom remembers her. "Où sont les neiges d'antan?" is a cliché of Romanticism and is intentionally "over-the-top." Amanda's slightly ridiculous behaviour both in the scene quoted and in her later "jonquil" speech reminded me of the histrionic performing of actresses like Lilian Gish in the early silent films. This gave me the idea of presenting the screen legends in the form of silent film subtitles. While neither the acting style nor the conventions of silent film subtitles were originally meant to be funny, time has made them so. In "memory" they appear laughable. Certainly audiences in Armidale found the use of these legends amusing and therefore were induced to see Amanda in the ironic light of a silent film heroine! The use of silent film subtitles also seemed to reflect Tom's obsession with the movies. When Williams's stage instructions are read without awareness of their ironical overtones they do indeed appear banal. Once one moves from page to stage however their theatrical power is easily realized. A few examples should suffice to illustrate the subtlety of Williams's use of screen legends. In scene 6 Laura learns that the gentleman caller is none other than Jim O'Connor, the boy she has silently loved from schooldays! Now if this is played realistically without any ironic comment it becomes the most clichéd piece of coincidental nonsense. This is precisely what happens in Williams's Acting Edition:

LAURA: Mother!
AMANDA: What's the matter now? (*Re-entering room.*)
LAURA: What did you say his name was?
AMANDA: O'Connor. Why?
LAURA: What is his first name?
AMANDA: (*Crosses to armchair R.*) I don't remember—Oh
    yes, I do too—it was—Jim! (*Picks up flowers.*)
LAURA: Oh Mother, not Jim O'Connor?

There is not a note of irony here—all we have is soap-opera. In Williams's Reading Edition we have the following:

LAURA: (*With an altered look.*) What did you say his
    name was?
AMANDA: O'Connor.
LAURA: What is his first name?
AMANDA: I don't remember. Oh yes, I do. It was—Jim!
    (LAURA *sways slightly and catches hold of a chair.*)
    (LEGEND ON SCREEN: "NOT JIM!")
LAURA: (*Faintly*) Not—Jim!
AMANDA: Yes, that was it, it was Jim! I've never known a
    Jim that wasn't nice! (*The music becomes ominous.*)

In this version the soap-opera cliché is not made at all realistic. Rather Williams heightens the level of cliché to a point where it is parody. This is the ironic parodic view of Tom's memory and we experience both its pathos and its bathos. "Not Jim!" like the later legend "Terror!" are so overtly melodramatic that they almost certainly cause a chuckle and the ominous music is a perfect parodic "gilding of the lily."

Laughter is constantly encouraged by Williams's stage devices. A most obvious example occurs when Tom groans:

You know it don't take much intelligence to get yourself into a nailed up coffin, Laura. But who in hell ever got himself out of one without removing one nail? (*As if in answer, the father's grinning photograph lights up. The scene dims out.*)

In Armidale we used the larger than life picture of the "telephone man who fell in love with long distance" and when the spot on the picture came up on the otherwise darkened stage, it was always greeted with a sympathetic laugh. Often the stage devices that Williams employs are to make the audience laugh in order that they may not weep. Tom's ironic defence against the pain he feels at Laura's situation is almost always laughter. He knows that there is no solution to Laura's problems. No gentleman caller will save her. To emphasize this, in my production I cast an actress who could play Laura as physically not very attractive and as mentally slightly retarded. The brace on her leg was really only a symbol of her being a psychic cripple like Williams's sister Rose who was the model for Laura. No magic "adjustment" as occurred in the film of *The Glass Menagerie* was possible for this Laura. The scene where this Laura, replete with "gay deceivers" padding her brassiere and overdressed in one of Amanda's old ball-gowns examines herself in a mirror, would have been a total tear-jerker without the irony supplied by both the screen legend and the sound effects:

(LEGEND ON SCREEN: THIS IS MY SISTER: CELEBRATE HER WITH STRINGS! MUSIC PLAYS.)

Tom's voice, heard through the caption, holds back the pain and possible tears by the use of rather bitter irony.

Perhaps the most effective stage device that Williams uses to prevent his audiences from empathising too readily with the characters from Tom's past is The Screen Image. The finest example of this relates to Jim, the gentleman caller. The device allows us to see Jim's character in relation to the whole action of the play which concerns man's need for "illusions."

In scene 5 Amanda and Tom have discussed callers in general and Jim in particular. Amanda has checked him out as a prospective suitor for Laura. Despite Tom's attempts to control Amanda's fantasies this "nice, ordinary, young man" with freckles is turned by her into an ideal suitor for her daughter. His going to night school means for Amanda that

he has visions of being advanced in the world! Any young man who studies public speaking is aiming to have an executive job some day!

Scene 5 ends with an uncomprehending Laura being asked by an elated Amanda to wish on the moon. A romantic moon is projected as a screen image and the scene dims out to the accompaniment of a violin! Every signal to the audience presages disaster for Amanda's plan. Tom's honest description of Laura's psychic limitations has already shown the audience that she lives "in a world of her own." The screen image of the moon and the sentimental violin, when juxtaposed with Tom's view of Laura, ironically emphasize the fantasy world of Amanda with her pathetic wish for "Happiness! Good Fortune!" At the end of this scene everything is set up for the catastrophe of Jim's visit. It was at this point that I placed the Interval. The idea was to keep the audience in suspense.

Scene 6 begins with Tom giving another of his narrator speeches. As this mirrors the opening of scene 1, I again had him enter from the auditorium. He immediately begins to talk about Mr. O'Connor and a screen image of the expected gentleman caller appears. This is a picture of Jim, the high-school hero. The audience has by now almost come to know Jim, partly because of Tom's description of him but mainly because they have seen pictures of him before. The first picture was in scene 2 at the point when Amanda first gets the idea of marrying Laura off to some unsuspecting gentleman caller:

> (SCREEN IMAGE: JIM AS HIGH SCHOOL HERO BEARING A SILVER CUP.)

In this early picture the actor attempted to show some of the "tremendous Irish good nature and vitality with the scrubbed and polished look of white chinaware" that Tom refers to at the beginning of scene 6.

The second picture of Jim that the audience sees occurs at the beginning of scene 3 when Tom humorously observes:

> Like some archetype of the universal unconscious, the image of the gentleman caller haunted our small apartment. . . .
> (SCREEN IMAGE: A YOUNG MAN AT THE DOOR OF A HOUSE WITH FLOWERS.)

The audience in Armidale immediately recognised that the young man was the same fellow who had earlier appeared carrying a silver cup.

The third picture of Jim appears in scene 5. The scene has opened with the gently blasphemous legend "Annunciation" which of course presages a visitation. Jim may not be God-Almighty, but he does later state: "I'm Superman!" In scene 5 the picture of Jim is a repetition of the one in scene 3:

TOM: We are going to have one.
AMANDA: What?
TOM: A gentleman caller!
(*The annunciation is celebrated with music.* AMANDA *rises.*)
(IMAGE ON SCREEN: A CALLER WITH A BOUQUET.)

The picture of Jim, the high-school hero that opens scene 6 is therefore the fourth time we have seen this confident young man. Before his actual arrival however there is one more image of him that ironically cuts this walking example of the American Dream down to size. As someone who "was shooting with such velocity through his adolescence that you would logically expect him to arrive at nothing short of the White House by the time he was thirty," Jim has in fact not lived up to his dreams of success. Tom points out:

> His speed had definitely slowed. Six years after he left
> High School he was holding a job that wasn't much better
> than mine. (SCREEN IMAGE: THE CLERK.)

The image we had of Jim in my production was of a harrassed looking clerk checking off a clipboard list amid row upon row of shoeboxes. This image, following the four earlier pictures of Jim in his glory always produced laughter from the audience and prepared the way for them to see that Jim's image of himself which occurs later in scene 6:

(IMAGE ON SCREEN: EXECUTIVE AT HIS DESK.)

was as laughably inflated as Amanda's earlier view of him as an executive. The effect on the audience of Jim's actual "visitation," having seen five pictures of him, was electrifying. With one audience of high-school students the appearance of Jim produced excited mutterings on the theme of "Here he is!" What the screen images had done was to make Jim become what Williams intended him to be, namely "the long-delayed but always expected something that we live for." Instead of being the Redeemer, Jim turns out unintentionally to bring hell rather than heaven to the Wingfield home. The stage devices—the nonrealistic use of lighting, the music, the legends and the screen images, all combine to help the audience to realize that Jim is just as much a dreamer as either Laura or Amanda. As Stein has delightfully pointed out:

> Jim's attempt to play the modern saviour is an abysmal

failure. In the after dinner scene, he offers Laura the sacrament—wine and "life-savers," in this case—and a Dale Carnegie version of the Sermon on the Mount—self-help rather than divine help—but to no avail.

The film version and the Acting Edition of *The Glass Menagerie* are both pushed toward realism. Often in productions of the Reading Edition directors follow the critical objections of writers like Gassner and Styan and cut the expressionistic/plastic staging devices from the script. The result is that a realistic portrayal of a particular family is produced. The play becomes a sensitive portrayal of the plight of a few pathetic individuals. This leads to a devaluation of Williams's work. It leads critics like Falk to see Amanda as "an escapist like her daughter . . . [who] also lives unhappily in her cocoon of dreams."

What Williams's nonrealistic stage techniques help an audience to see is that there is in the play no one single absolute reality to which characters can adjust. Jim O'Connor, who in the film version clearly represented reality and helped Laura snap out of her inferiority complex, is shown in the Reading Version to be living in his own Glass Menagerie world. His belief in the illusions of the prevailing American Dream with its success myth are undermined by his actual achievement. He is not an executive but a clerk. It is only in fantasy that his beliefs succor him.

> JIM: *Knowledge*—Zzzzzp! *Money*—Zzzzzp! *Power!* That's the cycle democracy is built on.

The action of Williams's play then is not about a group of misfits who fail to adjust to reality. Jim is "an emissary from *a* world of reality" not *the* world of reality. All the characters in the play live in private illusionary worlds. Williams is presenting an action that is making a universal statement about what he sees as the human condition. Amanda lives "vitally in her illusions" of a past age of jonquils and gentleman callers; Laura lives in a world of glass animals and old records; Jim lives in an illusory world of hopes of success and even Tom lives in the world of art. He escapes to the movies and into the world of writing.

What Esther Merle Jackson has called "The Broken World of Tennessee Williams" can only be realized on stage if the idea of a single absolute and "normal" reality is rejected. This is especially true of *The Glass Menagerie*. Each character in the play creates his or her own subjective reality as a defence against the "horror at the heart of the meaninglessness of existence." The only absolute in Williams's dramatized vision of reality is death: "There is no way to beat the game of *being* as against *non-being*, in which non-being is the predestined victor on realistic levels." Against the awfulness of this absurd reality, symbolized in *The Glass Menagerie* by the alleys outside the Wingfield apartment, the individuals give their lives meaning by using their imaginations to create fragile glass menagerie worlds— worlds that are "truth in the pleasant disguise of illusion."

Given that Williams believes in a vision of reality that is so highly relativistic, in which "no man has a monopoly on right," it is not surprising that he has rejected realism as a means for expressing his vision. The solid mirror of external reality is suitable for expressing a vision of reality where truth is absolute, but not where there are as many truths as there are people. What is surprising is the way that so many critics and even more importantly, so many directors reject, or neglect to follow, Williams's stated nonrealistic intentions. Williams has argued that "truth, life, or reality is an organic thing which the poetic imagination can represent or suggest, in essence, only through transformation, through changing into other forms than those which were merely present in appearance." It seems wilful distortion on the part of critics and directors to neglect the use of the nonrealistic staging devices that facilitate the "transformation" Williams desires, in favour of producing a realistic slice-of-life that presents aspects of reality "merely present in appearance."

The Circle Closed: A Psychological Reading of *The Glass Menagerie* and *The Two Character Play*

R. B. Parker

"He thought he could create his own circle of light."
In the Bar of a Tokyo Hotel

On February 25, 1983, I was correcting galley proofs of a Twentieth Century Interpretations volume on *The Glass Menagerie* when it was announced over the radio that Tennessee Williams had died in a New York hotel, bizarrely choking on a plastic bottle-top while under the influence of barbiturates. A spate of eulogies followed. Walter Kerr called him "the greatest American playwright. Period"; and Marlon Brando affirmed more personally that Tennessee Williams "was a very brave man . . . he never lied or flunked. He told the truth as best he perceived it, and never turned away from things that beset or frightened him." I sadly added a last item to the chronology at the back of my anthology.

I had been asked to edit that collection of essays because, in casual chat with the general editor, I said it seemed to me perverse to reduce the heavy theatricalism of *The Glass Menagerie,* as most productions do, and particularly wrong to dismiss its film projections as awkward, pretentious, and jejune—as even sympathetic critics like Lester A. Beaurline and Gilbert Debusscher had recently maintained.

From *Modern Drama* 28, no. 4 (December 1985). ©1985 by the University of Toronto, Graduate Centre for Study of Drama.

There are two distinct versions of *The Glass Menagerie* in print. The Dramatists Play Service's Acting Edition is based on the version actually staged by Eddie Dowling in 1945 (and still preferred for most productions). This has no projections or mimed action, and the text shows considerable rewording, especially in the Amanda speeches and in Tom's "framework" speeches (that is, those speeches in which Tom-remembering introduces and comments on the play directly to the audience). The other version, known as the Reading Edition, published originally by Random House and currently by New Directions, is the one that Williams, having bowed to Dowling's pressure for changes in the performance text, nevertheless insisted be printed and has enshrined in his *Collected Theatre*. This does have the projections; much of the play's early business must be mimed (for example, in scene 1, the family is directed to mime eating with nonexistent knives, forks and food); and the wording is much more complex and ironically ambivalent than in the acting text. In particular, there is a certain self-conscious, overelaborate "poeticizing" quality in Tom's framework speeches, particularly at the end, which produces what is perhaps one of Williams's most characteristic effects as a theatre artist, the effect of self-conscious symbolism (let us call it) which can be seen at its fullest development in *Camino Real,* and which is also integral to the peculiar "memory play" effect he was pioneering in *The Glass Menagerie,* a point that will be returned to later.

To research background for the anthology, I visited the University of Texas at Austin in order to examine the big Williams archive that had recently been deposited in the Humanities Research Center there, only to be appalled at the sheer amount of material that confronted me. Williams was a compulsive writer: he spent four or five hours at his typewriter every morning, no matter where he was, partly as therapy but also as the one consistency in his otherwise anarchic life; and he was a compulsive rewriter, who explained to one of his interviewers:

> Finishing a play, you know, is like completing a marriage or a love affair. . . . You feel very forsaken by that, that's why I love revising and revising, because it delays the moment when there is this separation between you and the work.

He was apt to put the same material through many different forms: poem, short story, one-act play, full-length play (rewritten several times), novel, and film or television script; and he claimed that no work could be considered fixed until he had stopped working on it. Three years ago, the Texas material was only roughly sorted out by title; and, to compound confusion, in revising Williams had the habit of mixing altered pages with pages from earlier drafts that needed no change. There is thus a huge problem for some dedicated scholar in the future, sorting out the sequence of these textual alterations—especially when one remembers that the Texas archive will have to be collated with other Williams material at the Barrett Library of the University of Virginia and the mass of papers the playwright willed at his death to Harvard University.

From the pile of *Gentleman Caller* revisions (the original title of *Menagerie*) and related drafts of the short-story version, "A Portrait of a Girl in Glass," it became clear that the genesis of the play—and, more importantly, Williams's own emotional relationship to his material—were infinitely more complex than had hitherto been understood. Four impressions in particular stood out. In the first place, many of the discarded drafts were much more like what we have come to think of as typical Williams writing: that is, they were more sexually charged, more violent, and more blackly humorous (especially at Amanda's expense) than the final play. And the eventual omission of these elements perhaps explains Williams's own curious lack of enthusiasm for this, his most widely produced and best-loved play, the one that established his reputation. He scrawled on the cover of his final typescript: "The Glass Menagerie, a rather dull little play by Tennessee Williams"; and we find him writing to his friend Donald Windham in 1943: "'The Gentleman Caller' remains my chief work, but it goes slowly, I feel no overwhelming interest in it. It lacks the violence that excites me." Even after its phenomenal success, he warned *Time* magazine that in it: "I said all the nice things I have to say about people. The future things will be harsher."

In the second place, the drafts reveal two new aspects of the symbiotic relationship between the brother and sister (Tom and Laura). This relationship not only is more central to the play's action than might have been assumed from the critics' concentration on the mother (Amanda), but also is treated with a startling range of moods: in particular, with a considerable variety of attitudes to the Laura character, ranging all the way from quiet, stoic heroism at one extreme to sheer neurasthenic bitchiness at the other.

In the third place, Williams clearly had great difficulty in devising a suitable end. There are numerous drafts of both happy and sad conclusions, which seem to show that what he wanted intuitively was a complex *mixed* reaction to the end—mingling relief and guilt, bravado and regret, ruthlessness and gentle pity—for which he found it very difficult to create an adequate dramatic form. (He seems to have worked intuitively, trying to get the right "feel.") And finally, related to this problem, we find his experimenting in the drafts with various sorts of "frameworks" to contain the remembered incident of the gentleman caller, including one which I think is especially worth recalling in which Tom argues directly and a little abrasively with the audience about the truth of the memory he is presenting—an element more discreetly retained in the final play in such distancing devices as Tom's celebrated opening speech: "Yes, I have tricks in my pocket, I have things up my sleeve. . . . I give you truth in the pleasant guise of illusion."

Williams's solution was, of course, his virtual invention of the "memory play" form, which, as Paul T. Nolan has pointed out, differs from either a confessional format or the involuntary recall of stream-of-consciousness expressionism because in the "memory play" we not only see exclusively what the narrator consciously wants us to see, but also see it only in *the way* he chooses that we should. It is precisely here that the main interpretative problem of *The Glass Menagerie* lies. It is a problem both of "mood"—that is, the complex attitude that Tom-remembering has to the events he recalls—and of "tone"—that is, the slightly mocking, not wholly ingenuous stance that Tom seems to take to the audience, a stance that is much more subtle and ambiguous than the sentimental, poetic sincerity (lightened with a few wry laughs) that has determined the way of acting Tom-the-narrator since Eddie Dowling first created the role.

The key to both these problems lies in the ambiguity of Tom's attitude to Laura. This attitude is, of course, basically one of loving regret for having abandoned her; but we should remember that in the short story "A Portrait of a Girl in Glass," which is one of the alternative presentations of the same incident, there is a distinct, if guarded, hint of incestuous attraction between brother and sister. In the Reading Version of *The Glass Menagerie*, moreover, we have to cope with several film projections which seem to *mock* Laura's terror at Jim's advent and her hopelessness when he leaves; and we must also recognize the ruthlessly self-damaging implications of

Tom's final command, when he bids Laura blow out her candles to plunge not only herself but also Tom-remembering into the final stage blackout.

There are hints of complexity in the brother's remembrance of his relation to his sister, then, that seem directly linked to the very innovative "plastic theatre" devices of the staging (to use Williams's own terminology in the production notes to the play). I wish to argue, therefore, that implicit in the very structure of *The Glass Menagerie* is a connection between sex and art whose common denominator is a recognition and fear of solipsism—of consciousness turned in on itself, "inordinately possessed of the past" (as Williams has described his work in general), where theatre is not simply an emotional escape but also a form of introversion. Williams's "memory play" uses the box-within-box structure perfected by Pirandello as a comment on the self-referentiality of theatre; and its final effect is rather like that famous mime of Marcel Marceau in which a man trapped in a small box worms his way out of it only to find himself trapped in a bigger box outside. The angst of such introversion for the dramatist comes out at the end of Williams's essay "The Timeless World of a Play" (published originally with *The Rose Tattoo*), where he worries that

> unless [the playwright] contrives in some way to relate the dimensions of his tragedy to the dimensions of a world in which time is *included*—he will be left among his magnificent debris on a dark stage, muttering to himself.

This image of abandoned solipsism prefigures a play written at the end of Williams's career to which *The Glass Menagerie* is most intimately related, the play known variously as *The Two Character Play* and, more vividly, as *Out Cry*. Talking to Mike Wallace about things he had learned from psychoanalysis in the 1950s, Williams explained:

> A term I've come across lately is "infantile omnipotence. . . ." That is what we all have as babies. . . . All [the infant] has to do is cry out and it will be comforted, it will be attended to. All right. We grow up a little and we discover that the outcry doesn't meet this tender response always. . . . [The infant] meets a world which is less permissive, less tender and comforting, and it misses the maternal arms—the maternal comfort—and therefore, then, it becomes outraged, it becomes angry.

It is the contradictoriness of this emotion—its tenderness, need, re-
vulsion, and anger—that must be the focus of our concern.

II

Solipsism that exists in sibling love and solipsism that can result
when drama is used therapeutically come together very illuminat-
ingly in a play that Tennessee Williams first issued in 1967 with the
title *The Two Character Play*, then rewrote in 1971 and again in 1973
as *Out Cry*, only to revise it yet once more in 1975 under its original
title—which also happens to be the title of its play-within-the-play.

Though its implications were not probed, the relation of the
play to *The Glass Menagerie* was immediately recognized. Claudia
Cassidy, the reviewer whose praise had prevented Williams's backers
from closing *Menagerie* during its Chicago try-out, noted that:
"[Williams] said in *The Glass Menagerie*, 'This is a memory play.'
Well, in a sense so is *Out Cry*"; and another critic, Peggy Prenshawe,
saw the play as "in some ways like a sequel to *The Glass Menagerie*."
Williams himself regarded it as the masterpiece of the second half of
his career. "I think it is my most beautiful play since *Streetcar*," he is
reported as saying on the cover of the New Directions edition, "and
I've never stopped working on it. . . . It is a *cri de coeur*, but then all
creative work, all life, in a sense is a *cri de coeur*." And in his star-
tlingly frank *Memoirs*, on which he was working while he revised
Out Cry, he calls this play "the big one," the one "close to the mar-
row of my being," in which he was "very deeply emotionally involved." "I considered *Out Cry* a major work," he insists, "and its
misadventure on Broadway has not altered that personal estimate of
it." Moreover, he was not alone in this estimate; the play was also
highly regarded by his agent, Audrey Wood, and by several important theatre people, including Michael Redgrave and Hume Cronyn.
Of particular interest for us is the latter's enthusiastic comment that
"in a fashion, there was more revelation of Tennessee in that play
than in anything of his that I have ever read."

The action of the play is stripped down almost to allegory. An
actor-playwright, Felice Devoto, and his actress sister, Clare, find
themselves abandoned by their theatre company (who claim they are
insane) in an underground theatre in some unknown, icy northern
state, with a performance due before an animally antagonistic audience. There is a clear indication of incestuous feeling between the
two. Felice turns a ring on Clare's finger, we are told, as "a sort of
love making"; and after a crisis towards the end of the play, they

compulsively "embrace—like two lovers meeting after a long separation." Though Clare is unwilling to go on with the performance, Felice insists that they put on a play called *The Two Character Play*, that he is still in process of writing, arguing that they can ad lib when his text runs out. This play-within is also about a brother and sister, also called Felice and Clare, who live in the southern USA and are afraid to leave the family house where their astrologer father killed their mother for wanting to send him to the state asylum, then shot himself. The play-within has the brother and sister reminiscing about their childhood and recollecting their parents' murder-suicide: Clare is looking for the murder weapon, a revolver that Felice (who has also been in the state asylum) has hidden; and they make several abortive attempts to contact the outside world or leave the house, which they recognize as having become their "prison." Felice introduces improvisational material into the play which seems designed to make the brother and sister reenact their parents' tragic relationship, and Clare desperately keeps evading the implications of this, to a point, just before the end, of completely breaking out of the play-within illusion. The siblings then discover, however, that their audience have left the auditorium; there is no longer anyone backstage; the doors are locked; and the theatre, now also described as a "prison," is getting darker and colder. The only escape left to them is returning into the southern warmth of the play-within-the-play and completing its fatal action—which involves Clare finding the revolver, distracting Felice with soap-bubbles, then shooting him. When the moment comes, however, she finds she cannot go through with it; and Williams comments:

> In both the total play and the play within it, two desperately gallant but hopelessly deviant beings, find themselves, in the end, with no escape but self-destruction, which fails them too.

In the final version of the play (printed in volume 5 of Williams's *Collected Theatre*), Clare tries to shoot Felice and cannot; then Felice tries to shoot Clare and finds it equally impossible; then, the stage direction tells us: "As they slowly embrace, there is total darkness in which THE CURTAIN FALLS." In his notes to the director for this version, Williams says:

> There may be no apparent sexuality in *The Two Character Play,* and yet it is actually the *Liebestod* of the two charac-

ters from whom the title derives. This fact should be recognized by the director and players, but then it should be
forgotten.

Another interesting difference between the final version and the earlier ones is that the sister in the framework (or envelope) play is now
made much less attractive than Clare in the play-within: instead of
being just fatigued, she is "stoned"; she is coarse and violent in language; and she scratches her brother's face.

That there should be several versions of the play is typical of
Williams's method of composition, as was noted earlier; but in this
case there seems also an obsessional element involved. Clare says of
her brother's script: "As for *The Two Character Play*, when he read it
aloud I said to myself, 'This is his last one, there is nothing more
after this!'"; and Williams himself told Tom Buckley: "If I live, it'll
be my best play. . . . In any case, it'll be my last long play." And
though, in fact, he lived to write several plays subsequently, it is
nonetheless true that in *The Two Character Play* Williams, who was at
the end of his tether, was trying to grapple directly with the two
central and interlocked experiences of his life: his ambiguous, near-
incestuous love for his schizophrenic sister Rose; and his compulsive
need for theatre as personal escape and therapy.

We may turn at this point, then, to consider the relation of *The
Two Character Play* to Williams's life and other work, circling back
through these to a reconsideration of neglected aspects of *The Glass
Menagerie*.

III

First, it is necessary to understand the circumstances in which
Williams wrote the later play. It was a product of the late 1960s and
early 1970s, when he was struggling through a period of almost total
psychic collapse brought on by his lover's death, drugs, and theatrical failure. (He later called the 1960s his "stoned age.") In the later
1950s he had undergone a year of intense psychoanalysis with Dr.
Lawrence Kubie, who tried to get him to abandon writing and to
change his sexual orientation. Not surprisingly, this treatment
merely led him even deeper into depression, so another of his doc-
tors, Dr. Max Jacobson, introduced him to "speed" (amphetamines
injected into the vein) to get him writing again and to counteract the
sleeping-pill and alcohol habits Williams had already contracted. "I

took sedation every night," says Williams, "and every morning I took something related to speed, so that I could still write." Inevitably the result was a catastrophic breakdown. Physically, this took the form of disorientation and frequent falls (as Clare falls down in the final version of the play); mentally, Williams was haunted by a constant unspecific terror ("The fierce little man with a drum within the rib cage," Felice calls it), resulting in bizarre late-night dashes to the nearest airport and paranoid letters to the newspapers about attempts to kidnap or murder him. Finally, in 1969 his younger brother Dakin committed him to three months' severe "cold-turkey" treatment at a psychiatric clinic in St. Louis, a traumatic experience reflected in *The Two Character Play* by references to "State Farm" and "that forbidden word . . . confinement." "Confinement has always been the greatest dread of my life," he says in *Memoirs*; "that can be seen in my play *Out Cry*."

The other factor crucial to the play, besides this state of breakdown, is Williams's complex relation to his sister, Rose, and his guilt about her institutionalizing and frontal lobotomy. The epigraph for *The Two Character Play* comes from the Song of Solomon 4:12, "A garden enclosed is my sister . . . a spring shut up, a fountain sealed"; and here, of course, is the play's most obvious overlap with *The Glass Menagerie*'s Laura, whose glass unicorn—the symbol of virginity—has its horn snapped off.

The biographical circumstances which lie behind *Menagerie* are so well known that the barest summary of them should suffice. The Williams parents were badly mismatched: a rowdy shoe salesman and the prim daughter of an Episcopalian minister; and Tom and Rose, two years his elder, were raised by Mrs. Williams in their grandfather's various southern rectories while C. C. Williams was on the road. Tom was apparently a normal, aggressive little boy until he fell victim to a severe bout of diphtheria at the age of four, which led to introversion and almost complete reliance on the companionship of Rose, at that time a lively, imaginative little girl. In *Memoirs*, Williams says:

> I may have inadvertently omitted a great deal of material
> about the unusually close relations between Rose and me.
> Some perceptive critic of the theatre made the observation
> that the true theme of my work is "incest." My sister and I
> had a close relationship, quite unsullied by any carnal

knowledge. As a matter of fact, we were rather shy of each other, physically. . . . And yet, our love was, and is, the deepest in our lives and was, perhaps, very pertinent to our withdrawal from extrafamilial attachments.

This imaginative symbiosis was intensified by the family's move to St. Louis, where the father's firm had given him a desk job. Both children were horrified by the ugliness and violence of the big Midwestern city, by the relative poverty in which they now had to live—compared to the gentility of their grandfather's rectories—and by their father's noisy, overbearing presence; and Williams (on whom his father was particularly hard) more and more took refuge in his sister's white-painted bedroom with its window-shade drawn down against the ugliness of the alley outside (according to "Portrait of a Girl in Glass," a savage chow here used to corner and kill cats), where Rose's collection of fragile glass animals represented for her brother "all the small and tender things that relieve the austere pattern of life and make it endurable to the sensitive." However, as Williams recounts in an early short story, "The Resemblance between a Violin Case and a Coffin" (*Hard Candy* [1954]), this close relationship was disrupted by Rose's arrival at puberty, when—the story suggests—Williams may also have transferred his sexual feelings for his sister to the handsome boy with whom she took her music lessons. Interestingly, an article in *New York*, July 25, 1983, records that at the time of his death Williams was working on a screen-play called *Ladies' Choice*, based on this short story and on another, entitled *Completed*, about the very same event. In part 3 of one of his poems, "Recuerdo," he movingly records:

> At fifteen my sister
>   no longer waited for me,
> impatiently at the White Star Pharmacy corner
>   but plunged headlong
>   into the discovery, Love!
> Then vanished completely—
> for love's explosion, defined as early madness
> consumingly shone in her transparent heart for a season
> and burned it out, a tissue-paper lantern!
>   . . . My sister was quicker at everything than I.

According to *Memoirs*, Rose was a normal, if highly sexed, girl who was driven into schizophrenic withdrawal by the combination of her mother's prudery and her father's appalling social blunders; but Williams also bitterly blamed himself. "It's not very pleasant to look back on that year [1937]," he writes, "and to know that Rose knew she was going mad and to know, also, that I was not too kind to my sister." He tells of her tattling on a wild party he gave during their parents' absence, in resentment of which he hissed at her on the stairs, "I hate the sight of your ugly old face!" leaving her stricken and wordless, crouched against the wall. "This is the cruelest thing I have done in my life, I suspect," he comments, "and one for which I can never properly atone." Later that year Rose was institutionalized, when, according to her brother Dakin, she became "like a wild animal," till their mother authorized one of the first frontal lobotomy operations in America, rendering Rose "a mental vegetable."

As soon as he became successful, Williams took the greatest possible care of his sister: he kept a black-hung shrine to her in his bedroom; he moved her in 1982 to a house next to his own in Key West, under the care of an elderly cousin; and besides the *Ladies' Choice* script he was working on at the time of his death, one of his very last plays, called *Kirche, Kuchen and Kinder,* is a two-hander about "Miss Rose" and "the Man"—Tennessee Williams himself. Ironically, the connection has continued even after death: Williams was not buried at sea near the spot where Hart Crane jumped to his death in the Caribbean, as he had requested, but rests finally in a cemetery in St. Louis with a vacant plot next to his own waiting for the body of Rose.

It was surely this relationship that helped to establish Williams's homosexuality, with its strong sadomasochistic quality reflecting his belief that love the "Comforter" is also always and inevitably a "Betrayer." Brother-sister incest themes run throughout his work. Besides the four titles already noted, it appears in an early one-act verse play, *The Purification,* where a wife is murdered by her husband for incest with her brother, then both men kill themselves. *You Touched Me!,* a full-length play written in collaboration with Donald Windham, changes its D. H. Lawrence source to show an adopted son (who may, in fact, be the real son) marrying his "sister" after a shy and curiously childlike courtship where he talks of her broken dolls, of little silver bells, and of how gentle his hands are going to be. In the one-act *The Last Goodbye,* it is the introverted brother who cannot leave the family house after he has driven away his desperate, promiscuous sister with the lament: "What happens to kids when they grow up?" And most obviously, in *Suddenly Last Summer* (written in 1958, after Williams's year in psychoanalysis), a young woman is threatened with lobotomy for revealing her male "cousin's" homosexuality to his possessive mother.

Closely related to incest are two other recurrent themes: an obsession with pubescent girls and a delight in androgynous young men. Among the former, one may cite the screen-play *Baby Doll;* Heavenly, the fifteen-year-old whose memory Chance Wayne pursues so despairingly in *Sweet Bird of Youth* (leading to her sterilization and his emasculating); Kilroy's passion for the ever-renewed virginity of Esmeralda in *Camino Real;* and Shannon's self-destructive pursuit of nymphets in *The Night of the Iguana.* Williams's last book of poems was called *Androgyne, mon Amour,* and in an interview with *Playboy* (April 1973), he explained that what attracted him to young men was always an androgynous quality about them. In *The Two Character Play,* the names Felice and Clare seem to have been chosen partly because they are androgynous, and Clare describes Felice himself as having shoulder-length hair like a woman.

Such themes and such a sensibility relate Williams to the late Romantic and Symbolist writers, and it seems appropriate, therefore, that Laura's odd nickname, "Blue Roses" (a play upon "pleurosis"), has been traced to "L'Idéal," a poem from Baudelaire's *Fleurs du Mal.* The destructive incest of brother and sister is explored in many later Romantic works, most notably perhaps in Poe's *The Fall of the House of Usher* and Villiers de l'Isle-Adam's *Axël* (where Axël and Sara are described as two halves of one androgynous whole); and androgyny is a striking aspect of much turn-of-the-century art. But, even beyond this, Williams also shares the "decadent" sensibility's idea of art as a complementary stasis to sexual involution, a related way of resisting the devouring rush of time (as in his essay "The Timeless World of a Play"). One of the shrewder comments made about *Out Cry,* in fact, was Clive Barnes's prophecy that the play "will one day be regarded as one of the most remarkable symbolist plays of the late twentieth century."

IV

This prophecy leads to the next point, however, because we should not jump at too simple a Freudian sexual "solution" to the experience at the root of Williams's art before we consider as well his attitude to writing and, specifically, to theatre. He began to write at the age of eleven, when Rose ceased to be his "other self," and art had always been a form of personal therapy for him. "It was a great act of providence," he says, "that I was able to turn my borderline psychosis into creativity." Writing became the main constant in his life, basic to his sense of identity: "If we're not artists, we're nothing," says Felice, "magic is the habit of our existence"; and Williams claimed that this literally saved his life at the time of his first breakdown in 1935—when, incidentally, Rose showed the earliest sign of her own insanity by coming to his room to say: "Let's die together."

The danger of living so intensely by imagination, however, is solipsism; and Williams was always aware of and acutely alarmed by this tendency in himself. Dakin tells a revealing anecdote of his brother aged seventeen, on his first trip to Europe, when Williams had a "waking nightmare" which left him shaking and drenched with sweat, "terrified by the thought of thought, by the concept of the process of human thinking, as a mystery in human life, and it made him think he was going mad."

Besides reflecting the closeness of his link to Rose, therefore, the Clare-Felice relationship in *The Two Character Play* can also be seen in terms of a split in Williams's own existentialist self-consciousness. In psychological terms, it is not just Freudian "incest" that is involved, but also the Jungian problem of "psychic individuation," the self-consciousness's struggle to reconcile its sense of separate selves. In Williams, this struggle habitually took the form of a sexual split within himself. "I am Blanche DuBois," he claimed about his most famous heroine; "I think that more often I have used a woman rather than a man to articulate my feelings." Discussing his youthful tendency to blush, he said: "Somewhere deep in my nerves was imprisoned a young girl"—a comment he elaborated in an interview with the *New York Times* in 1975, in which he said he believed there was no person living who "doesn't contain both sexes. Mine could have been either one. Truly, I have two sides to my nature." And a recurrent pattern in Williams's last plays is an unhappily symbiotic couple used as a symbol for the prison of introverted imagination, the ego unable to escape the twin circles of self and family: Miriam and Mark in *In the Bar of a Tokyo Hotel*, for instance; Leono and her brother in *Small Craft Warnings;* or the institutionalized Zelda in *Clothes for a Summer Hotel*, accusing Scott Fitzgerald of having drained away her life to create his art.

This pattern is especially interesting in relation to some of the most recent psychological thinking about incest. Whereas for classical Freudians incest is wholly a sexual issue, for more recent theorists it is a taboo necessary for psychic individuation—the individual's need to separate himself from an overriding attachment to what the jargon calls his primary "love object" (usually the mother, or mother-substitute), with psychosis arising when the boundaries between self and "love object" are not maintained (as Felice and Clare finish each other's sentences and constantly employ "chiasmus"—a grammatical mirror effect—in their sentence structures). The theory is that, at the time when a young child is trying to separate his consciousness of self from his identification with his mother, he becomes prey to a double anxiety: anxiety at losing his sense of identity if he loses his "love object" (hence his constant, obsessive returns to her), yet equally his fear of not attaining full individuation if he does not have the necessary aggression to break away—what the New York psychoanalyst Margaret S. Mahler calls "man's eternal struggle against both fusion and isolation." This anxiety happens at the toddler age, but can recur again and again at later stages; and we remember that at the time of Williams's childhood illness and later in his isolation in St. Louis, Rose was the only person in the world who accepted him without reservation, who shared a secret imaginative world with him, who loved him, and whom he could love with all the emotional intensity of a deeply sensitive and beleaguered child; and this love was Williams's main form of self-assertion against the world before he began to write. Moreover, according to Otto Rank, the *"Geschwester-Komplex"* in later life is particularly a revolt against existential isolation and awareness of death; the idealized sister then becomes a necessary symbol of immortality, the sole guarantee against death of the body and the impermanence of desire which threaten life with meaninglessness.

When it is put into this perspective, one can see that *The Two Character Play* has a Freudian play-within-the-play about imaginative incest, in which the family is the "prison," and the Jungian framework play of solipsism in art, an obsessive recollection and restructuring of the past, in which the theatre is the "prison." In *The Two Character Play*, Felice and Clare share both solipsisms, but in *The Glass Menagerie* earlier, the sister is left to destroy herself in the prison of the home, while the brother, I suggest, is caught just as surely in the prison of memory, his own imaginative inability not to relive the past.

This situation throws doubt on the way Tom Wingfield remembers, however, that arbitrariness of the "memory play" form on which Nolan remarked. As Prenshawe says about the problem of Williams's own use of art as therapy:

> Viewing art as an extension of the artist, either for what he is or what he needs, leads solipsistically back to the mortal and flawed being that the artist seeks to transcend. . . . Tom Wingfield casts a magical web over experience, transforming the ordinary and ugly and even painful, into a thing of beauty. But undermining . . . [his] transformations of life into art is [his] . . . (and [his] creator's) lurking doubt that the vision is wholly truthful.

V

Let us return, therefore, for a last, brief look at *The Glass Menagerie,* to see how what we can now recognize as a recurrent Williams pattern was already adumbrated in the situation and technique of his first successful play, so many years before.

To start with, the pattern throws light on the purpose behind Tom's "memory play." This "memory play" is often spoken of as an exorcism of the past, but, if so, it is no more than an *attempt* to exorcise. It is better understood as an obsessive reliving of the experience in an attempt to come to terms with it, which recurs to Tom against his will, as is clear from the end of his last speech: "Oh, Laura, Laura, I tried to leave you behind me, but I am more faithful than I intended to be." This is the pattern of Yeats's *Purgatory* or Sartre's *Huis clos* (for which Williams expresses admiration in *Memoirs*): the pattern of guilty reenactment.

Similarly, understanding of the pattern throws light on the element of overelaborateness, of slightly false posturing, poeticizing and self-conscious symbol making in some of Tom's framework speeches, especially towards the end. This element is admitted by Williams himself in *Memoirs*:

> I agree with Brooks Atkinson that the narrations are not up to the play. . . . Thank God, in the 1973 television version of it, they cut the narrations down. There was too much of them.

Yet, as Thomas L. King demonstrates, in the Reading Edition Tom's soliloquies

> alternate between sentiment and irony, between mockery and nostalgic regret, and they all end with an ironic tag, which, in most cases, is potentially humorous. They show us the artist manipulating his audience, seeming to be manipulated himself to draw them in, but in the end resuming once more his detached stance.

The very sense of "forcing" in the style makes us question the integrity of the speaker, alerting us to ambivalences in his attitude: his wish to justify himself as well as to grieve, his surrender to emotion but at the same time his ironic, self-defensive distancing from it.

And this sense of ambivalence, of wishing to withdraw and deny *at the same time* as to relive and accept, is particularly important for the much maligned projection device. Like the theatricalism of having the characters mime eating or Tom playing the first scene "as though reading from a script," projections such as the sailing vessel with the Jolly Roger which accompanies Tom's dreams of adventure (and links them, incidentally, to Jim's high-school swaggering in *The Pirates of Penzance*) serve to maintain an ironic distance between the early Tom-within-the-play and the later Tom-remembering, through whose presentation the audience must willy-nilly experience the play.

Moreover, this device achieves more than reducing the sentimental "nostalgia" which Williams admits in his production notes is the "first condition" of *The Glass Menagerie;* its black, occasionally jarring, not-so-funny humour (that in *Out Cry* Williams calls the "jokes of the condemned") also throws light on Tom's mocking, self-protective attitude to the pain he is involuntarily reliving. The exaggeration of projections such as "Annunciation," when the gentleman caller is announced, or "The Sky Falls," when Amanda hears that he is already engaged, is like the obtrusive playing of the Ave Maria by *"the fiddle in the wings,"* in that it both mocks Amanda's self-dramatizing and *also* shows us Tom trying to distance himself from the pain of his feelings of guilt about her.

Moreover, the theatricalism has a further effect. It creates a gap between the commentary of Tom-remembering and the audience's own emotional reactions to events, like that Texas draft in which Tom is made to argue about the play directly with the audience. And this appears most disturbingly in relation to Laura, who is otherwise a wholly sympathetic character without the dimension of absurdity that is clear in Amanda, Jim, and Tom himself. She is given such a parodic dimension, however, by projections like "NOT Jim!" or "Terror," "Ah" followed by "Ha," or "Gentleman caller waving goodbye—gaily," prompting Gilbert Debusscher to protest in his *York Notes* (1982) on the play:

> The legends would appear [to be] unintentionally ludicrous and would introduce a dismaying note of parody into the most poignant scenes. . . . Fortunately, Eddie Dowling . . . sensed how damaging the projections might prove in a play as delicate as *The Glass Menagerie,* and ordered them out.

But suppose this effect was not "unintentional," that the parody was deliberate! Does this not, in fact, reflect very accurately the self-lacerating aggression necessary for the individual who is trying to free himself from too close an emotional dependence on his central "love object?" And is this not what the whole play is about? In his production notes, Williams says:

> When a play employs unconventional techniques, it is not, or certainly shouldn't be, trying to escape its responsibility of dealing with reality, or interpreting experience, but is actually or should be attempting to find a closer approach, a more penetrating and vivid expression of *things as they are.* (Italics added.)

This consideration brings us finally to a reassessment of the end of the play: Tom's command, "Blow out your candles, Laura—and so goodbye," that plunges both of them into the dark. We have seen a similar effect at the end of *The Two Character Play* described by Williams as a *Liebestod* (but one that must not be blatant); and we must associate it with the "holy candles" said to glisten in Laura's eyes, with the fact that the candlesticks came from a church that was struck by lightning, and with the way that the final blackout reenacts Tom's previous betrayal of the family to darkness when he misappropriated the electricity money—just as his deliberate smashing of his glass at the end, in exasperation at his mother, recapitulates his earlier, accidental smashing of Laura's glass animals and Jim's disfigurement of the unicorn (both light and glass being symbols for

Laura herself, who is described as resembling "transparent glass touched with light"). If we take into acount, furthermore, the fact that Tom bids Laura put out her own candles, surely what we are faced with at the end is not *only* a regretful, tender and pathetic mood (though, of course, we do have that, very powerfully), but also a ruthless reenactment of Tom's original violation of his sister's trust, a loving, necessary murder like Othello's "Put out the light," in which the Comforter has turned Betrayer but in doing so has had to kill part of himself? Williams comments on similar ambivalences in the ruthless love of Maggie the Cat by quoting August Strindberg: "They call it love-hate, and it hails from the pit."

There is a shadow round the delicate *Glass Menagerie*, then, that the charm and pathos of the play should not obscure for us. Recognition that it is there makes for a more complex psychological study and also "places" the play more solidly and centrally within Williams's characteristic view of human nature and particularly of love. Appreciating the work of Harold Pinter, Williams commented:

> The thing that I've always pushed in my writing—that needed to be said over and over—[is] that human relations are terrifyingly ambiguous. If you write a character that isn't ambiguous, you are writing a false character, not a true one.

This ambiguity extends to the Tom-Laura relationship, which, far more than the cruder, more obvious relation to Amanda, determines the play's tone and mood; and its main key lies in the expressionistic dramaturgy of *The Glass Menagerie*—the various devices that ironize, distance, and complicate emotional response—which is so often ignored or unjustly dismissed. That dramaturgy anticipates from the first the obsessions and techniques with which Tennessee Williams's career concluded.

Chronology

1911	Born Thomas Lanier Williams in Columbus, Mississippi.
1911–18	Lives with mother and sister, Rose, and maternal grandparents, as father is often away on business. They move often, finally settling in St. Louis, Missouri.
1927	Wins prize for essay "Can a Good Wife Be a Good Sport?" then published in *Smart Set* magazine.
1928	Visits Europe with grandfather. First story published in *Weird Tales:* "The Vengeance of Nitocris."
1929	Enters University of Missouri. Wins honorable mention for first play, *Beauty Is the World*.
1931	Father withdraws him for flunking ROTC at university. Works at father's shoe company.
1935	Released from job after illness and recuperates at grandparents' house in Memphis, where his play *Cairo! Shanghai! Bombay!* is produced.
1936–37	Enters and is later dropped from Washington University, St. Louis. Enters University of Iowa. First full-length plays produced: *The Fugitive Kind* and *Candles to the Sun*. Prefrontal lobotomy performed on sister, Rose.
1938	Graduates from University of Iowa.
1939	First uses name "Tennessee" on "The Field of Blue Children," published in *Story* magazine. Travels from New Orleans to California to Mexico to New Mexico to St. Louis. Awarded $1,000 Rockefeller grant. Begins new full-length play, *Battle of Angels*.
1940	Moves to New York to enroll in advanced playwrighting seminar taught by John Gassner at The New School.

1941–43	Takes various jobs in Provincetown, New York, Macon (Georgia), Jacksonville (Florida), and St. Louis. Begins *The Gentleman Caller* (later *The Glass Menagerie*). Works at MGM as scriptwriter.
1944	Awarded $1,000 by the National Institute of Arts and Letters for *Battle of Angels*. *The Glass Menagerie* opens in Chicago on December 26.
1945	*The Glass Menagerie* opens in New York; wins New York Critics' Circle Award.
1946	*27 Wagons Full of Cotton and Other Plays* published.
1947	*A Streetcar Named Desire* opens in New York. *Summer and Smoke* opens in Dallas, Texas; wins second New York Critics' Circle Award and Pulitzer Prize.
1948	*Summer and Smoke* opens in New York. *American Blues: Five Short Plays* published. *One Arm and Other Stories* published.
1950	*The Roman Spring of Mrs. Stone*, a novel, published. *The Rose Tattoo* opens in Chicago.
1951	*The Rose Tattoo* opens in New York; wins the Antoinette Perry (Tony) Award for best play. Film version of *A Streetcar Named Desire*, screenplay by Williams and Oscar Saul, released.
1953	*Camino Real* opens in New York.
1954	*Hard Candy: A Book of Stories* published.
1955	*Cat on a Hot Tin Roof* opens in New York; wins third New York Critics' Circle Award and second Pulitzer Prize.
1956	*Baby Doll*, a film, released, and *In the Winter of Cities*, poems, published. Father dies. Williams begins psychoanalysis.
1957	*Orpheus Descending* opens in New York.
1958	*Garden District (Something Unspoken* and *Suddenly Last Summer)* opens off-Broadway. Film version of *Cat on a Hot Tin Roof* released.
1959	*Sweet Bird of Youth* opens in New York.
1960	*Period of Adjustment* opens in New York.
1961	*The Night of the Iguana* opens in New York.
1962	Film version of *Sweet Bird of Youth* released. A one-act version of *The Milk Train Doesn't Stop Here Anymore* presented in Spoleto, Italy, at the Festival of Two Worlds.

1963	Full-length version of *Milk Train* opens in New York. Period of depression begins after death of his lover Frank Merlo.
1964	Film version of *The Night of the Iguana* released.
1966	*Slapstick Tragedy (The Mutilated* and *The Gnädiges Fraulein)* opens in New York.
1967	*The Two Character Play* opens in London. *The Knightly Quest: A Novella and Four Short Stories* published.
1968	*Kingdom of Earth (The Seven Descents of Myrtle)* opens in New York.
1969	*In the Bar of a Tokyo Hotel* opens off-Broadway. Converts to Roman Catholicism. Stays three months in hospital in St. Louis after nervous collapse.
1970	*Dragon County: A Book of Plays* published.
1971	Revised version of *The Two Character Play* called *Out Cry* opens in Chicago.
1972	*Small Craft Warnings* opens off-off-Broadway.
1973	*Out Cry* (a third revision of *The Two Character Play*) opens in New York.
1974	*Eight Mortal Ladies Possessed: A Book of Stories* published.
1975	Receives the National Arts Club gold medal for literature. *Moise and the World of Reason*, a novel, is published. *The Red Devil Battery Sign* opens in Boston. Fourth version of *The Two Character Play* opens off-off-Broadway. *Memoirs* published.
1976	Revised *Red Devil* opens in Vienna.
1977	*Vieux Carré* opens in New York.
1978	*Creve Coeur* opens in Charleston, South Carolina. *Where I Live: Selected Essays* published.
1979	*A Lovely Day for Creve Coeur*, revised version of *Creve Coeur*, opens in New York.
1980	*Clothes for a Summer Hotel* opens in Washington, D.C. Mother dies.
1981	*A House Not Meant to Stand* opens in Chicago. *Something Cloudy Something Clear* opens in New York.
1982	Receives honorary degree from Harvard University.
1983	Dies in February.

Contributors

HAROLD BLOOM, Sterling Professor of the Humanities at Yale University, is the author of *The Anxiety of Influence, Poetry and Repression,* and many other volumes of literary criticism. His forthcoming study, *Freud: Transference and Authority,* attempts a full-scale reading of all of Freud's major writings. A MacArthur Prize Fellow, he is general editor of five series of literary criticism published by Chelsea House. During 1987–88, he served as Charles Eliot Norton Professor of Poetry at Harvard University.

ROGER B. STEIN teaches in the departments of English Literature and Rhetoric at the State University of New York at Binghamton.

LESTER A. BEAURLINE teaches in the Department of English at the University of Virginia, Charlottesville. He is the author of *Jonson and Elizabethan Comedy: Essays in Dramatic Rhetoric* and has also written on John Dryden.

NANCY M. TISCHLER teaches in the Department of English and Humanities at Pennsylvania State University in Middletown.

ELMO HOWELL teaches English at Memphis State University.

GILBERT DEBUSSCHER teaches English and American literature at the University of Brussels in Belgium. He is the author of *Edward Albee: Tradition and Renewal* and numerous articles on contemporary American theater.

FRANK DURHAM is the author of *Elmer Rice.* He has taught at the University of South Carolina.

CHARLES S. WATSON teaches English at the University of Alabama. He is the author of *Antebellum Charleston Dramatists.*

SIGNI FALK has taught English at Coe College and is the author of books on Williams and Archibald MacLeish as well as numerous short stories and articles.

C. W. E. BIGSBY is Reader in American Literature in the School of English and American Studies at the University of East Anglia in Norwich. His books include *Dada and Surrealism, Confrontation and Commitment: A Study of Contemporary American Drama, 1959–1966,* and *The Second Black Renaissance: Essays in Black Literature,* as well as studies of Tom Stoppard, Joe Orton, and Edward Albee.

GEOFFREY BORNY writes on dramatic production.

R. B. PARKER is Professor of English and currently Dean of Arts and Vice Provost of Trinity College at the University of Toronto. His research areas are Renaissance English drama and modern American and Canadian drama. He edited an anthology of essays on *The Glass Menagerie* in 1983.

Bibliography

Adler, Thomas P. "The Search for God in the Plays of Tennessee Williams." *Renascence* 26 (1973): 48–56.

Albee, Edward. "Which Theater Is the Absurd One?" In *The Modern American Theater*, edited by A. B. Kernan. Englewood Cliffs, N.J.: Prentice-Hall, 1967.

Atkinson, Brooks. "Theatre: Early Williams." *The New York Times*, 22 November 1956.

Bentley, Eric. *In Search of Theatre*. New York: Knopf, 1953.

———. *The Life of the Drama*. New York: Atheneum, 1964.

Berkowitz, Gerald. "The 'Other World' of *The Glass Menagerie*." *Players* 48, no. 4 (1973): 150–53.

Bigsby, C. W. E. *A Critical Introduction to Twentieth-Century American Drama*. vol 2; *Tennessee Williams, Arthur Miller, Edward Albee*. Cambridge: Cambridge University Press, 1984.

Bloom, Harold, ed. *Modern Critical Views: Tennessee Williams*. New Haven, Conn.: Chelsea House, 1987.

Brandt, George. "Cinematic Structure in the Works of Tennessee Williams." In *American Theatre*, Stratford-upon-Avon Studies 10, edited by J. R. Brown and B. Harris, 163–88. London: E. Arnold, 1967.

Braun, E. "*The Glass Menagerie*." *Plays and Players* 27 (January 1980): 29–30.

Brooks, Charles B. "The Comic Tennessee Williams." *The Quarterly Journal of Speech* 44 (1958): 275–81.

Broussard, Louis. *American Drama: Contemporary Allegory from Eugene O'Neill to Tennessee Williams*. Norman: University of Oklahoma Press, 1962.

Brustein, Robert. *Seasons of Discontent: Dramatic Opinions, 1959–1965*. New York: Simon & Schuster, 1965.

———. "Why American Plays Are Not Literature." In *Writing in America*. New Brunswick, N.J.: Rutgers University Press, 1960.

Cate, Hollis L., and Delma E. Presley. "Beyond Stereotype: Ambiguity in Amanda Wingfield." *Notes on Mississippi Writers* 3, no. 3 (1971): 91–100.

Clayton, John Strother. "The Sister Figure in the Plays of Tennessee Williams." *Carolina Quarterly* 12 (1960): 47–60.

Clurman, Harold. *The Divine Pastime*. New York: Macmillan, 1974.

———. *Lies Like Truth*. New York: Macmillan, 1958.

———. "Theatre." *The Nation* 199 (August 10, 1964): 60.

Cohn, Ruby. *Dialogue in American Drama*. Bloomington: Indiana University Press, 1971.

Corrigan, Mary Ann. "Memory, Dream and Myth in the Plays of Tennessee Williams." *Renascence* 28 (1976): 155–67.

Debusscher, Gilbert. *York Notes on Tennessee Williams: The Glass Menagerie*. London: Longman, York Press, 1982.

Dervin, Daniel A. "The Spook in the Rain Forest: The Incestuous Structure of Tennessee Williams' Plays." *Psychocultural Review* 3 (1979): 153–83.

Dickenson, Hugh. "Tennessee Williams: Orpheus as Savior." In *Myth on the Modern Stage*, 278–309. Urbana: University of Illinois Press, 1969.

Donahue, Francis. *The Dramatic World of Tennessee Williams*. New York: Ungar, 1964.

Falk, Signi. *Tennessee Williams*. New York: Twayne, 1961.

Fedder, Norman J. *The Influence of D. H. Lawrence on Tennessee Williams*. The Hague: Mouton, 1966.

Free, William J. "Camp Elements in the Plays of Tennessee Williams." *The Southern Quarterly* 21, no. 2 (1983): 16–23.

Fritscher, John J. "Some Attitudes, and a Posture: Religious Metaphor and Ritual in Tennessee Williams's Query of the American God." *Modern Drama* 13 (1970): 201–15.

Ganz, Arthur. "The Desperate Morality of the Plays of Tennessee Williams." *American Scholar* 31 (1962): 278–94.

Gardner, R. H. *The Splintered Stage: The Decline of the American Theatre*. New York: Macmillan, 1965.

Gassner, John. "Broadway in Review." *Educational Theatre Journal* 11, no. 2 (1959): 122–24.

———. *Masters of the Drama*. New York: Dover, 1954.

———. "Tennessee Williams: Dramatist of Frustration." *College English* 10 (1948); 1–7.

Gilman, Richard. *Common and Uncommon Masks: Writings on the Theatre—1962–1970*. New York: Random House, 1971.

Gunu, Dawey Wayne. "The Various Texts of Tennessee Williams' Plays." *Educational Theatre Journal* 30, no. 3 (1978): 368–75.

Jackson, Esther Merle. *The Broken World of Tennessee Williams*. Madison: University of Wisconsin Press, 1965.

———. "The Problem of Form in the Drama of Tennessee Williams." *CLA Journal* 4 (1960): 8–21.

Jennins, Robert. "Tennessee Williams: A Candid Conversation with the Brilliant, Anguished Playwright." *Playboy*, April 1973, 69–84.

Jones, Robert Emmet. "Tennessee Williams's Early Heroines." *Modern Drama* 2 (1959): 211–19.

Kerr, Walter. *God on the Gymnasium Floor and Other Theatrical Adventures*. New York: Simon & Schuster, 1969.

King, Thomas L. "Irony and Distance in *The Glass Menagerie*." *Educational Theatre Journal* 25, no. 2 (1973): 207–14.

Krutch, Joseph Wood. "Modernism." In *Modern Drama*. Ithaca, N.Y.: Cornell University Press, 1953.

Leavitt, Richard Freeman, ed. *The World of Tennessee Williams*. London: Allen, 1978.

Lewis, Allan. *American Plays and Playwrights of the Contemporary Theatre*. New York: Crown, 1965.

Lumley, Frederick. *New Trends in 20th Century Drama: A Survey since Ibsen and Shaw*. 3d ed. New York: Oxford University Press, 1967.

Magid, Marion. "The Innocence of Tennessee Williams." *Commentary* 35, no. 1 (January 1963): 34–43.

Mannes, Marya. "The Morbid Magic of Tennessee Williams." *The Reporter* 12 (May 19, 1955): 41–44.

Nathan, George Jean. *The Theatre Book of the Year, 1944–45*. Rutherford, N.J.: Fairleigh Dickinson University Press, 1945.

Navone, John. "The Myth and Dream of Paradise." *Studies in Religion* 5 (1975): 152–61.

Nelson, Benjamin. *Tennessee Williams: The Man and His Work*. New York: Obolensky, 1961.

Nolan, Paul T. "Two Memory Plays: *The Glass Menagerie* and *After the Fall*." *The McNeese Review* 17 (1966): 27–38.

Parker, Brian. "The Composition of *The Glass Menagerie*: An Argument for Complexity." *Modern Drama* 25 (1982): 409–22.

Parker, R. B., ed. *Twentieth Century Interpretations of* The Glass Menagerie: *A Collection of Critical Essays*. Englewood Cliffs, N.J.: Prentice-Hall, 1983.

Pavlov, Grigor. "A Comparative Study of Tennessee Williams' *The Glass Menagerie* and 'Portrait of a Girl in Glass.'" *Annuaire de l'Université de Sofia, Faculté des Lettres* (1968): 111–13.

Popkin, Henry. "The Plays of Tennessee Williams." *Tulane Drama Review* 4, no. 3 (March 1960): 45–64.

Presley, Delma E., and Hari Singh. "Epigraphs to the Plays of Tennessee Williams." *Notes on Mississippi Writers* 3, no. 2 (1970): 2–12.

Robey, Cora. "Chloroses—Pâles Roses and Pleurosis—Blue Roses." *Romance Notes* 13 (1971): 250–51.

Rowland, J. L. "Tennessee's Two Amandas." *Research Studies of Washington State University* 35, no. 4 (December 1967): 331–40.

Sagar, K. M. "What Mr. Williams Has Made of D. H. Lawrence." *Twentieth Century* 168 (1960): 143–53.

Stang, Joanne. "Williams: 20 Years after *Glass Menagerie*." *The New York Times*, 28 March 1965.

Stanton, Stephen, ed. *Tennessee Williams: A Collection of Critical Essays*. Englewood Cliffs, N.J.: Prentice-Hall, 1977.

Styan, John. *Modern Drama in Theory and Practice: Realism and Naturalism*. Vol. 1. Cambridge: Cambridge University Press, 1981.

Tharpe, Jac L., ed. *Tennessee Williams: A Tribute*. Jackson: University Press of Mississippi, 1977.

Tischler, Nancy M. *Tennessee Williams: Rebellious Puritan*. New York: Citadel, 1961.

Traubitz, Nancy B. "Myth as a Basis of Dramatic Structure." *Modern Drama* 19 (1976): 55–66.

Tynan, Kenneth. "American Blues: The Plays of Arthur Miller and Tennessee Williams." *Encounter* 2, no. 5 (1954): 13–19.

Vowles, Richard B. "Tennessee Williams and Strindberg." *Modern Drama* 1 (1958): 166–71.

———. "Tennessee Williams: The World of His Imagery." *Tulane Drama Review* 3, no. 2 (December 1958): 51–56.

Weales, Gerard. *Tennessee Williams*. Minneapolis: University of Minnesota Press, 1965.

Williams, Tennessee. "On a Streetcar Named Success." *The New York Times*, 30 November 1947.

———. "The Timeless World of a Play." In *Perspectives on Drama*, edited by James L. Calderwood and Harold E. Toliver. New York: Oxford University Press, 1968.

———. *Where I Live: Selected Essays*. New York: New Directions, 1978.

Young, Stark. "*The Glass Menagerie*." *The New Republic* 112 (April 16, 1945): 505.

Acknowledgments

"*The Glass Menagerie* Revisited: Catastrophe without Violence" by Roger B. Stein from *Western Humanities Review* 28, no. 2 (Spring 1964), © 1964 by the University of Utah. Reprinted by permission.

"*The Glass Menagerie:* From Story to Play" by Lester A. Beaurline from *Modern Drama* 8, no. 2 (September 1965), © 1965 by A. C. Edwards. Reprinted by permission of *Modern Drama*.

"*The Glass Menagerie:* The Revelation of Quiet Truth" (originally entitled *"The Glass Menagerie"*) by Nancy M. Tischler from *Tennessee Williams: Rebellious Puritan* by Nancy M. Tischler, © 1961 by Nancy M. Tischler. Reprinted by permission of The Citadel Press.

"The Function of Gentlemen Callers: A Note on Tennessee Williams's *The Glass Menagerie*" by Elmo Howell from *Notes on Mississippi Writers* 2, no. 3 (Winter 1970), © 1970 by *Notes on Mississippi Writers*. Reprinted by permission of *Notes on Mississippi Writers*.

"Tennessee Williams's Unicorn Broken Again" by Gilbert Debusscher from *Revue Belge de Philologie et d'Histoire* 49 (1971), © 1971 by *Revue Belge de Philologie et d'Histoire*. Reprinted by permission.

"Tennessee Williams: Theatre Poet in Prose" by Frank Durham from *South Atlantic Bulletin* 36, no. 2 (March 1971), © 1971 by South Atlantic Modern Language Association. Reprinted by permission of *South Atlantic Bulletin*.

"The Revision of *The Glass Menagerie:* The Passing of Good Manners" by Charles S. Watson from *The Southern Literary Journal* 8, no. 2 (Spring 1976), © 1976 by *The Southern Literary Journal*. Reprinted by permission.

"The Southern Gentlewoman" by Signi Falk from *Tennessee Williams*, 2d ed., by Signi Falk, © 1978 by G. K. Hall & Co. Reprinted by permission of G. K. Hall & Co., Boston.

"Celebration of a Certain Courage" (originally entitled "Tennessee Williams") by C. W. E. Bigsby from *A Critical Introduction to Twentieth Century American*

Drama. Vol. 2, Tennessee Williams, Arthur Miller, Edward Albee by C. W. E. Bigsby, © 1984 by C. W. E. Bigsby. Reprinted by permission of the author and Cambridge University Press.

"The Two Glass Menageries: Reading Edition and Acting Edition" (originally entitled "*The Glass Menagerie:* An Examination of the Effects on the Meaning that Result from Directing the Reading Edition as Opposed to the Acting Edition of the Play") by Geoffrey Borny from *Page to Stage: Theatre as Translation,* edited by Ortrun Zuber-Skerritt, © 1984 by Editions Rodopi B. V., Amsterdam. Reprinted by permission.

"The Circle Closed: A Psychological Reading of *The Glass Menagerie* and *The Two Character Play*" by R. B. Parker from *Modern Drama* 28, no. 4 (December 1985), © 1985 by the University of Toronto, Graduate Centre for Study of Drama. Reprinted by permission of *Modern Drama.*

Index